THE
END TIMES

THE
END TIMES

Prophecies of Coming Changes

Includes prophecies and predictions from

THE BIBLE—EDGAR CAYCE

NOSTRADAMUS—THE HOLY MOTHER

JOHN VAN AUKEN

A SIGNET BOOK

SIGNET
Published by New American Library, a division of
Penguin Putnam Inc., 375 Hudson Street,
New York, New York 10014, U.S.A.
Penguin Books Ltd, 80 Strand,
London WC2R 0RL, England
Penguin Books Australia Ltd, Ringwood,
Victoria, Australia
Penguin Books Canada Ltd, 10 Alcorn Avenue,
Toronto, Ontario, Canada M4V 3B2
Penguin Books (N.Z.) Ltd, 182–190 Wairau Road,
Auckland 10, New Zealand

Penguin Books Ltd, Registered Offices:
Harmondsworth, Middlesex, England

Published by Signet, an imprint of New American Library,
a division of Penguin Putnam Inc. Published by arrangement with A.R.E.
Press. For information address A.R.E. Press, 215 67th Street, Virginia Beach,
VA 23451-2061.

First Signet Printing, December 2001
10 9 8 7 6 5 4 3 2 1

 REGISTERED TRADEMARK—MARCA REGISTRADA

Printed in the United States of America

CONTENTS

INTRODUCTION

As a topic for study, prophecy is both fascinating and frustrating. As you will see in the pages that follow, it can rivet your attention by opening up your awareness to the greater forces at work in the universe. At the same time, however, it is sometimes hard to decipher, couched as it is in archaic or obscure metaphors, and is often gloomy, since most of it seems to be doom and disaster. Prophecy implies that the future is preordained. Otherwise how could the seers predict what is to come? Yet most of us want to believe that it is we who determine our future through free will choice, not fate. But then unforeseen, even cataclysmic, events come out of nowhere to alter lives forever. Are these events predictable? If we knew what was to come, could we alter our destiny? Believers in prophecy say that we can.

When I first wrote this book in 1994, it was in response to the many writers and speakers in recent times who expressed troubling ideas about coming major earth changes, including predictions of everything from massive earthquakes to devastating shifts in the earth's poles. But prophecies such as these are not coming from only mystics and psychics. Today we even have scientists publishing increasingly upsetting predictions about the movements of our planet's tectonic plates, which could change landscapes and oceans forever. Add political prognosticators to the list of prophets, and we find a future filled with even more danger and change.

I decided to investigate these ideas for my own edification. I was surprised to find many modern and ancient prophecies that did appear to forecast major changes for our little blue planet. Of all the sources of these prophecies, I found four that I thought represented the largest and best body of material: the Bible; the great "sleeping prophet," Edgar Cayce; Nostradamus (and with him I have included the works of Bishop Malachy and the Monk of Padua); and the apparitions of the Virgin Mary, the mother of Jesus.

However, when I delved into the material more deeply, I found that few of the prophecies of earth changes could be published without including the broader context in which they were presented. For example, as I studied the Bible, it became clear that an overarching theme runs from Genesis through to the Revelation that may not be commonly understood by most followers of biblical prophecies, including Jews, Christians and Muslims, each of whom considers themselves to be the children of Abraham.

So I found it impossible to focus exclusively on earth-change prophecies without including their context or background. Thus this became a book not just about earth changes, but about prophecies of the "End Times." Or as the angel Gabriel calls it in the Book of Daniel, "the time of the end." (Dan. 8:19) What is the time of the end? Based on the prophecies that follow, it is not the end of the world, but the end of a long era or age, and the beginning of a new one. This is not a book about doom but about new hope after much needed change is accomplished. However, it is not just a book of optimism or philosophy either. I've included all the hard predictions of significant earth changes, changes that have the potential to take many lives and change many countries, continents and oceans. My intention is not to alarm people. Not all prophecies should be taken literally or as fate.

Some predictions may be a metaphor—for a shift in consciousness, for example—while others may not occur due to the intervention of human or divine will. My intention is to share what I've learned about these prophecies so that you the reader can come to your own conclusion.

Much of what is contained here can be viewed positively if we understand what life is really about. According to the prophecies in this book, far larger forces are at work than we might fully comprehend. Today's events are the direct result of past events. Edgar Cayce taught the validity of reincarnation. The circumstances of an individual today are influenced by its soul's prior activities and thoughts. It is not well known, but Christianity contains teachings about the influence of the "preexistence of the soul" on present life situations. Most prophets see our free will as existing in the midst of destiny—destiny being the effects of prior free will choices—so that present free will decisions determine future conditions. If this is so, then the choices and actions of the present life will affect us in the next life.

The same concept can be applied on a more macro level. Consider that nations and races are, in fact, soul groups. These groups would also *collectively* have a preordained destiny, one that is based in their past actions as a group. Thus the human race as a whole is fated in some fashion because of the choices we have made over the millennia.

And what of today? What about the small but terrible wars that still occur around the world, the terrorists attacks that have killed so many and created so much upset and bitterness, the global tensions in the name of religion, and the volcanic and earthquake activity that has recently done so much damage to towns and cities? Is it all part of a pattern? This pattern of change may have been set on its course a very long time ago. Much of the prophecy in this book will show that the current world situation is the result of previous, even ancient, circumstances.

This idea is nowhere as clear as when you consider the physical earth. The geological activity of the earth—earthquakes or volcanic eruptions—is very simply the result of forces set into motion eons ago. Scientists say that the activity is caused by the breakup of an ancient supercontinent or single landmass that they call Pangaea (meaning in Greek "all lands"). As it broke up, it divided into seven major plates that ultimately became nine large plates and a number of smaller ones, which form our continents and oceanic floors. These plates and their movements account for today's volcanic and earth-quake destiny.

As our earth's geological history illustrates, understanding prophecy may involve compre-hending the forces that were set in motion in ancient times, and considering how we, as hu-mans, respond to those forces. Throughout this book you will see that a spiritual response is called for. Does such a response mean we can change our destiny? Or are we all living out a destiny that was determined long ago?

In this book I hope we will get a better sense of these forces, not simply for knowledge's sake, but that we might direct our destiny to better tomorrows.

John Van Auken
1 October 2001

1

THE PROPHECIES
OF THE BIBLE

Biblical prophecies have proved difficult to interpret. This is because of their strange imagery and an intentional effort to obscure their meaning from the profane and the curious. The imagery in these prophecies comes from a deeper level of consciousness, thus requiring us to get to that level of consciousness before understanding is realized. Some of the messages are holistic, yet we strive to interpret them linearly. Some messages deal with the microcosm, but we strive to interpret them in the macrocosm. Nevertheless, the promise is:

Matt. 7:7–8 Ask and it will be given to you; seek and you will find; knock and the door

will be opened to you. For everyone who asks
receives; he who seeks finds; and to him who
knocks, the door will be opened.

I have also found that the biblical stories
and prophecies are difficult to understand if
one doesn't first realize that what we call
"man" or humans were originally "gods" or
spirits. Here are two statements from the Bible,
Old and New Testament, that bear witness to
this:

Ps. 82:6   I said, "You are gods; you are all
sons of the Most High."

John 10:34   Jesus answered them, "Is it not written in your Law, 'I have said you are gods'?"

The children of God were created and lived
in the heavens, or in the consciousness of God,
before they began to live in the flesh and the
earth. This is important to remember when trying to understand the predictions in the scrip-
tures.

There were *two* creations in Genesis. The first
(Gen. 1:26–27) was when we were created in the
image of God, which is *spirit*—"God is Spirit,"
John 4:23–24. Then, we were created again (Gen.
2:5–7) from the dust of the earth, or flesh. Now

there are two aspects to us, one spirit or godly and the other flesh or human. Here are those passages from Genesis:

Gen. 1:26–27 *So God created man in his own image, in the image of God he created him; male and female he created them.*

Gen. 2:4–8 This is the account of the heavens and the earth when they were created. When the Lord God made the earth and the heavens—and no shrub of the field had yet appeared on the earth and no plant of the field had yet sprung up, for the Lord God had not sent rain on the earth *and there was no man to work the ground*, but streams came up from the earth and watered the whole surface of the ground—*the Lord God formed the man from the dust of the ground and breathed into his nostrils the breath of life, and the man became a living being.*

Now the Lord God had planted a garden in the east, in Eden; and there he put the man he had formed.

Notice after we were created in Genesis 1 in the image of God (i.e., spirit), there was still "no man to work the ground." This was because we were not physical, not human or in the flesh, yet. As the last line indicates, God had not "formed" the man yet. Then a different level of

God, called the *Lord God* (Yahweh Elohim) created us a second time, now in the flesh—"from the dust of the earth."

Later, the Lord God divides the man-woman into separate male and female beings. At this point in the creation story, we were still immortal beings that lived in direct contact with the Lord God.

When we keep in mind that each being is both a godling and a human—or in biblical terms, a "son/daughter of God" and a "son/daughter of man"—then we can better understand why the biblical stories and prophecies are the way they are.

THE CURSE

If one reads carefully, the *first* biblical prophecy is given by the Lord God to Adam and Eve as they leave the Garden and the presence of the Lord. At this point, the godlings had descended out of their heavenly consciousness and completely into physical consciousness and human bodies. This was not meant to be, but since they used their free will to make it so, they had to go through it. In this next passage, the Lord God is speaking to our earthly selves. The Lord God does not want us to stay forever in the earth, and so He has cursed the earth, that it will not give us ultimate satisfaction and contentment.

Gen. 3:14–19 So the Lord God said to the serpent, "Because you have done this, cursed are you above all the livestock and all the wild animals! You will crawl on your belly and you will eat dust all the days of your life.

"And I will put enmity between you and the woman, and between your offspring and her offspring; he [*i.e., her offspring*] will crush your head, and you will bruise his heel."

To the woman He said, "I will greatly increase your pains in childbearing; with pain you will give birth to children. Your desire will be for your husband, and he will rule over you."

To Adam He said, "Because you listened to your wife and ate from the tree about which I commanded you, 'You must not eat of it,' cursed is the ground because of you; through painful toil you will eat of it all the days of your life.

"It will produce thorns and thistles for you, and you will eat the plants of the field.

"By the sweat of your brow you will eat your food until you return to the ground, since from it you were taken; for dust you are and to dust you will return."

Entry of the children of God into the physical world was not part of the great plan. But since the children chose the flesh over the spirit, they were then cursed to struggle through the realm of flesh until they chose the spirit and the realm of the Garden consciousness. Eventually the woman would produce an offspring that would crush the serpent's head, even as its evil bruises the Messiah's heel. This prophecy of the Messiah is important and will appear throughout the biblical prophecies. In the meantime, life in the earth will be hard for all concerned: serpent, woman and man.

Gen. 3:21–24 The Lord God made garments of skin for Adam and Eve and clothed them.

And the Lord God said, "The man has now become like one of us, knowing good and evil. He must not be allowed to reach out his hand and take also from the Tree of Life and eat, and live forever."

So the Lord God banished him from the Garden of Eden to work the ground from which he had been taken.

After He drove the man out, He placed on the east side of the Garden of Eden cherubim and a flaming sword flashing back and forth to guard the way to the Tree of Life.

Now we, the celestial, immortal children of God, have become predominantly terrestrial and mortal. We no longer have access to the Tree of Life. That is, not until we reach the end of this great journey described in the last book of the Bible, the Book of the Revelation. Here we find that the Tree of Life has been given back to the children, who may eat from it freely, and may drink the water of life freely. The story spans the loss of the Garden in Genesis to the "new heaven" and "new earth" of the final chapters in the Revelation:

Rev. 21:1–6 *Then I saw a new heaven and a new earth, for the first heaven and the first earth had passed away, and there was no longer any sea.*

I saw the Holy City, the new Jerusalem, coming down out of heaven from God, prepared as a bride beautifully dressed for her husband.

And I heard a loud voice from the throne saying, *"Now the dwelling of God is with men, and He will live with them. They will be His people, and God Himself will be with them and be their God.*

"He will wipe every tear from their eyes. There will be no more death or mourning or crying or pain, for the old order of things has passed away."

He who was seated on the throne said, "I am making everything new!" Then He said, "Write this down, for these words are trustworthy and true."

He said to me: "It is done. I am the Alpha and the Omega, *the Beginning and the End*. To him who is thirsty I will give to drink freely from the spring of the Water of Life."

Rev. 22:1–5   Then the angel showed me *the River of the Water of Life*, as clear as crystal, flowing from the throne of God and of the Lamb down the middle of the great street of the city.

On each side of the river stood *the Tree of Life*, bearing twelve crops of fruit, yielding its fruit every month. *And the leaves of the Tree are for the healing of the nations.*

No longer will there be any curse. The throne of God and of the Lamb will be in the city, and His servants will serve Him.

They will see His face, and His name will be on their foreheads.

There will be no more night. They will not need the light of a lamp or the light of the sun, for the Lord God will give them light. And they will reign for ever and ever.

Rev. 2:7   He who has an ear, let him hear what *the Spirit says. . . .* To him who overcomes, *I will give the right to eat from the Tree of Life, which is in the paradise of God.*

Obviously, it all ends happily ever after.

Why is it so important to understand these elements of the Bible before we can understand the prophecies? Because the prophecies are all about the journey from the fall from spirit and God's company, through the struggles with self-will and self-consciousness in the physical body

and the earth, then back to the full consciousness and attunement with the spirit and God.

Now when the Lord condemns or purges the
flesh or the earth, we understand that it is to
make room for the spirit, which is the true nature of every being. When the prophecies
scream for an end to earth by fire, flood, plague,
famine, and so on, we understand that it is a
cry for the rebirth of the spirit by subduing the
influences and demands of the flesh. When the
spirit is reborn, we unite these two aspects of
ourselves in a "new heaven" and a "new earth."
The curse is gone. All is new again. Every tear
wiped away, and joy is full.

THE END TIMES PROPHECIES

The first prophecy to use the term "End
Times" is found in the book of the prophet Daniel. It is the angel Gabriel that uses the term.

Dan. 8:15–19 While I, Daniel, was watching
the vision and trying to understand it, there before me stood one who looked like a man.

And I heard a man's voice from the Ulai [*a
river in Babylon*] calling, "Gabriel, tell this man
the meaning of the vision."

As he came near the place where I was standing, I was terrified and fell prostrate. "Son of

man," he said to me, "understand that the vision concerns *the time of the end*."

While he was speaking to me, I was in a deep sleep, with my face to the ground. Then he touched me and raised me to my feet.

He said: "I am going to tell you what will happen later in the time of wrath, because the vision concerns the appointed *time of the end*."

Clearly, Gabriel is saying that Daniel's vision is about "the time of the end." He goes on to tell Daniel just how long it will be until the End Time.

Dan. 7:25 He [*the earthly ruler*] will speak against the Most High and oppress His saints and try to change the set times and the laws. The saints will be handed over to him for a time, times and half a time.

We might ask, "Why are the saints handed over to the earthly ruler for a time, times and half a time?" Remember, the flesh and the earth are now integral portions of our total being. We are the earthly ruler—both in our own bodies and out among the world. Therefore God is allowing this newly acquired portion of our being to reign for a time, hoping that it will seek reunion with God rather than continue its self-seeking, earthly ways. But a time to end this matter has been set.

Dan. 12:6–7 "How long will it be before these astonishing things are fulfilled?" The man clothed in linen, who was above the waters of the river, lifted his right hand and his left hand toward heaven, and I heard him swear by him who lives forever, saying, "It will be for *a time, times and half a time.* When the power of the holy people has been finally broken, all these things will be completed."

Why must the power of the "holy people" be broken before all these things are completed? Because in the Garden, we chose the flesh over the spirit, self-interests over God's interests. The penalty was loss of the spiritual, i.e., the holy, and to live in the cursed flesh/earth until we chose to rebirth the spirit and reunite with God. Stern? Yes. Cruel? Not if you consider that our present nature is an *acquired* one that limits ourselves and God's ability to communicate with us. God's curse is holding a firm position to keep us from completely losing everything we were meant to be. As Jesus cried, "And now, Father, glorify me in your presence with the glory *I had with you before the world began.*" (John 17:5, my italics)

In Genesis we see the beginning of our duality in the two children that Adam and Eve conceived: Cain and Abel. In Hebrew, Cain literally means "acquired" and Abel means "breath." The breath is what the Lord God gave us when he made us of the earth—"the breath of life." And, as is seen in the Genesis story, God loves Abel. But the acquired one, Cain, is not pleasing to God. Yet when Cain confronts God over this, God replies: "If you do what is right, will you not be accepted? But if you do not do what is right, then sin is crouching at your door; it desires to have you, but you must master it." (Gen. 4:7)

As we'll see in the upcoming chapter on the Edgar Cayce prophecies, Cayce states that "the time, times and half a time" *are over*. This would mean, of course, that we are in the End Times. Here is what is prophesied:

Three sections of the Bible convey the major insights into the End Times: 1) Daniel's visions, 2) Jesus' teaching on the Mount of Olives, and 3) John's visions during the Revelation.

Since there is so much of it, repeated in slightly different ways in various books of the Bible, I will try to outline and highlight the key elements.

Let's begin with Daniel's visions and the Revelation. Then we'll look at Jesus' teaching on the Mount of Olives.

DANIEL'S FIRST VISION

Dan. 7:1–28 In the first year of Belshazzar king of Babylon, Daniel had a dream, and visions passed through his mind as he was lying on his bed. He wrote down the substance of *his dream*. Daniel said:

"In my vision at night I looked, and there before me were the *four winds* of heaven churning up the great sea.

"*Four great beasts*, each different from the others, came up out of the sea.

"The first was like *a lion*, and it had the wings of an eagle. I watched until its wings were torn off and it was lifted from the ground so that it stood on two feet like a man, and the heart of a man was given to it.

"And there before me was a second beast, which looked like *a bear*. It was raised up on one of its sides, and it had three ribs in its mouth between its teeth. It was told, 'Get up and eat your fill of flesh!'

"After that, I looked, and there before me was another beast, one that looked like *a leopard*. And on its back it had four wings like those of a bird. This beast had four heads, and it was given authority to rule.

"After that, in my vision at night I looked, and there before me was *a fourth beast*—terrifying and frightening and very powerful. It had large iron teeth; it crushed and devoured its victims and trampled underfoot whatever was left. It was different from all the former beasts, and it had ten horns.

"While I was thinking about the horns, there before me was *another horn, a little one*, which came up among them; and *three of the first horns were uprooted* before it. *This horn had eyes like the eyes of a man and a mouth that spoke boastfully.*

"As I looked, thrones were set in place, and the Ancient of Days took his seat. His clothing was as white as snow; the hair of his head was white like wool. His throne was flaming with fire, and *its wheels were all ablaze.*

"*A river of fire* was flowing, coming out from before him. Thousands upon thousands attended him; ten thousand times ten thousand stood before him. The court was seated, and *the books were opened.*

"Then I continued to watch because of the boastful words the horn was speaking. I kept looking until the beast was slain and *its body destroyed and thrown into the blazing fire.*

"(The other beasts had been stripped of their authority, but were allowed to live for a period of time.)

"In my vision at night I looked, and there before me was *one like a son of man,* coming with the clouds of heaven. He approached the Ancient of Days and was led into his presence.

"*He was given authority, glory and sovereign power; all peoples, nations and men of every language worshiped him. His dominion is an everlasting dominion that will not pass away, and his kingdom is one that will never be destroyed.*

"I, Daniel, was troubled in spirit, and the visions that passed through my mind disturbed me.

"I approached one of those standing there and asked him the true meaning of all this. So he told me and gave me the interpretation of these things:

" 'The four great beasts are four kingdoms that will rise from the earth.

" 'But the saints of the Most High will receive the kingdom and will possess it forever—yes, for ever and ever.'

"As I watched, this horn [i.e., the fourth beast] was waging war against the saints and defeating them, until the Ancient of Days came and pronounced judgment in favor of the saints of the Most High, and the time came when they possessed the kingdom.

"He gave me this explanation: 'The fourth beast is a fourth kingdom that will appear on earth. It will be different from all the other kingdoms and will devour the whole earth, trampling it down and crushing it.

" 'The ten horns are ten kings who will come from this kingdom. After them another king will arise, different from the earlier ones; he will subdue three kings.

" 'He will speak against the Most High and oppress his saints and try to change the set times and the laws. The saints will be handed over to him for a time, times and half a time.

" 'But the court will sit, and his power will be taken away and completely destroyed forever.

" 'Then the sovereignty, power and greatness of the kingdoms under the whole heaven will be handed over to the saints, the people of the Most High. His kingdom will be an everlasting kingdom, and all rulers will worship and obey him.'

"This is the end of the matter. I, Daniel, was deeply troubled by my thoughts, and my face turned pale, but I kept the matter to myself."

Daniel is viewing the sequence of beastly influences, and they rule a series of kingdoms on earth. Under the beasts are kings who rule the daily affairs of the kingdom, but supporting these kings are the beastly forces. The fourth beast is different from all the previous beasts, and the fourth kingdom is different from all the previous kingdoms. After the reign of ten kings, under the influence of the fourth beast, an eleventh king shall rise to power, different from all the others:

Dan. 7:25 He [*the eleventh king*] will speak against the Most High and oppress His saints and try to change the set times and the laws. The saints will be handed over to him for a time, times and half a time.

The fourth beast makes war against the saints and prevails! However, it is only until the Ancient of Days comes. Then the Ancient of Days judges the world and finds in favor of the saints of the Most High. Consequently, the saints inherit the kingdoms of the earth.

In the final chapter of the Book of Daniel, the prophet records another great vision of the End Times.

The angel says that during this period of struggle between the holy people and the earthly ruler, many will succeed in "purifying themselves and making themselves white and refined, but the wicked will grow in wickedness; none of the wicked will understand, but those who are wise will understand." The power of the holy people in the earth will be zero, wickedness will reign; then the Ancient of Days will move with the help of the archangel Michael and judge the earth, ultimately giving it over to the holy people.

In the Book of the Revelation, this pattern is repeated but with different symbols. A pure woman, "wrapped in the sun and standing on the moon" is pregnant with the Messianic ruler of the earth. She delivers the child who will rule the earth with an iron hand. The archangel Michael drives the dragon out of heaven.

Rev. 12:14 The woman was given the two wings of a great eagle, so that she might fly to the place prepared for her in the desert, where she would be taken care of for a time, times and half a time, out of the serpent's reach.

The dragon is so furious about this that he makes war with all her other offspring for generations. At this point in the Revelation, we see the rising up of the beast who will rule the earth and war against the children of God, just as we saw in Daniel. However, at the end of the stated time, times and half a time, the Holy One moves in and makes judgment upon the earth, separating the wicked from the seekers of God. And the seekers inherit the earth.

THE MICROCOSM AND MACROCOSM OF INTERPRETATION

Material that comes from the deeper consciousness of an individual can have two dimensions to it: microcosmic and macrocosmic. In other words, it reflects conditions *within* and *without*, or above and below, in heaven and in earth, in flesh and in spirit, in an individual and in the universe. This concept was first taught by Hermes in ancient Egypt. His teaching was stated: "As within so without, as above so below." It has been extensively elaborated upon in the Edgar Cayce readings, interpreting much of the Revelation with a *micro*cosmic understanding of this strange collection of images.[1] Carl Jung's ideas and examples have also added much to our understanding of how and why this occurs.[2]

If one doesn't acknowledge the duality of micro- and macrocosms (universes), one tends to look only outside of oneself for the interpretation. But much of what is being seen deals with the inner person, too.

Despite Daniel being in the dimension of phantoms and inner imagery, there is a humanlike person who comes to help Daniel with the interpretation. Daniel describes him as "one like a son of man." He tells Daniel that the four beasts in his dream are four kingdoms that will rise from the earth. But the saints of the Most High will ultimately "receive the kingdom and will possess it forever—yes, for ever and ever." Most of us would immediately take this to refer to the outer world of nations, governments and peoples. But it also relates to the inner world of organs, glands and cells—attitudes, emotions and thoughts. When one is in the spirit and the inner mind, the term "the earth" can mean the body as well as the world. When the humanlike person says, "the saints of the Most High," he can be speaking of those cells and organs within a body that have been rejuvenated with the spirit of health and life.

With this in mind, let's examine some of the elements of Daniel's vision—remembering that we are actually angelic, spiritual beings inside human, fleshly bodies.

"The four beasts" is an archetypal image

found throughout the Bible. Here are two more examples:

> Ezek. 1:10 Each of the four had the face of a man, and on the right side each had the face of a lion, and on the left the face of an ox; each also had the face of an eagle.

> Rev. 4:7 The first living creature was like a lion, the second was like an ox, the third had a face like a man, the fourth was like a flying eagle.

Notice the similarity in these beasts. In fact, both Ezekiel and John, though their visions are hundreds of years apart, see a man, lion, ox and eagle. Daniel sees a lion, bear, leopard and a terrible beast. Perhaps Daniel's fourth beast was like a man, but so viciously horrifying he could not call it such.

These beasts represent four lower, earthly forces *within* the human body, as well as four earthly powers in the outer world. Psalm 57:4 beautifully expresses our plight with these inner and outer forces: "I am in the midst of lions; I lie among ravenous beasts—men whose teeth are spears and arrows, whose tongues are sharp swords." Daniel's fourth beast has teeth that crush its victims. Perhaps the psalmist and Daniel were seeing the same beastly aspect of humanity—powerfully destructive forces within and around us.

St. John eventually sees another beast that incorporates all of Daniel's beasts into one: "The beast I saw resembled a leopard, but had feet like those of a bear and a mouth like that of a lion. The dragon gave the beast his power and his throne and great authority." (Rev. 13:2) This last sentence alludes to the ancient teaching that within each of us is a vital life force (kundalini), which is often symbolized as a serpent or dragon that moves through power centers within our bodies (chakras). Therefore John's comment that "the dragon gives the beast his power" fits well with these teachings. In fact, *chakras* is a Sanskrit word that means "wheels," and flaming wheels appear in Daniel's and Ezekiel's visions.

Dan. 7:9   As I looked, thrones were set in place, and the Ancient of Days took his seat. His clothing was as white as snow; the hair of his head was white like wool. His throne was flaming with fire, and *its wheels were all ablaze.*

Ezek. 1:15   As I looked at the living creatures, I saw a wheel on the ground beside each creature with its four faces.

Ezek. 1:20   Wherever the spirit would go, they would go, and the wheels would rise along with them, *because the spirit of the living creatures was in the wheels.*

Ezek. 10:13   I heard the wheels being called *"the whirling wheels."*

"Whirling wheels" is almost exactly how the ancients described the spiritual chakras in the human body. Each chakra is associated with attitudes, emotions and urges within every human. The Cayce readings say that the endocrine glands (pituitary, pineal, thyroid, thymus, adrenals, cells of Leydig, gonads—seven total) are at the core of the chakra forces. Cayce also says that when St. John sees the seven candles, the seven flames, the seven stars, and the seven churches, he is seeing these spiritual centers within himself. When these forces begin to catch fire with the movement of the life force, or élan vital, or kundalini energy, then they begin to whirl, and our godly selves begin to gain power again—for weal or woe.

The body is the ultimate temple of the Living God. John 2:21: "The temple [*Jesus*] had spoken of was his body." 2 Cor. 6:16: "We are the temple of the living God." All the imagery of the prophets includes visions into these inner processes. Out of the fleshly part of us will come the heavenly one. The battles, purgings and, ultimately, the Messiah will first come *within* each of us. Of course, it will all come in the outer world, as well.

THE GREAT AND TERRIBLE DAY OF THE COMING OF THE LORD

Because the coming of the higher self, or the godly self, is so profoundly overwhelming to the earthly self, it is often seen as a disaster for the lower self, or the human self. In a manner of speaking, it is the death of the lower self and the birth of the divine self. As the life force of the spirit begins to stir—or, as Daniel put it, "the four winds of heaven churning up the great sea"—the spiritual centers within the body begin to whirl, and the great powers are aroused. They are at first like beasts. "I was like a beast before Thee." (Ps. 73) But once subdued, they serve the Lord of the house.

In the Cayce material, the first four chakras are where most of our consciousness and energy exist. If we never control our urges or aspire to anything greater than gratification, then they become the four beasts that we are so familiar with: sex, possessiveness, violence and selfishness—the very stuff that every TV ad man knows will sell product. On the other hand, if we do control ourselves and aspire to more, then the life force creates higher energies in these centers, and it moves upward into the top three chakras. There it will be tested again, either to be found beastly or heavenly—and other battles ensue until the higher self is victorious.

It is a dangerous awakening. One can become a beast or an angel, depending upon what the dominant influence is. If it is self and gratification or glorification of self, then the beastly nature takes hold. If it is an attunement with the Creator and its ways, then the angelic one takes hold. And since others are in various stages of development with these energies, people can become beastly or angelic in their interaction with one another. The spirit of cooperation, mutual respect and a sense of the oneness of humanity, or the brotherhood/sisterhood, are needed to help all of us rise to higher levels.

Here's how the prophets have seen "the great and terrible day of the coming of the Lord." However, let's consider that the name *Lord* in this context is also referring to the overself, the godly self, that part that was created in the image of the Creator. From Isaiah to Peter we have remarkably similar and consistent imagery:

Isa. 13:6   Wail, for the day of the Lord is near;
it will come like destruction from the Almighty.

Isa. 13:9   See, the day of the Lord is coming—
a cruel day, with wrath and fierce anger—to
make the land desolate and destroy the sinners
within it.

Ezek. 30:3   For the day is near, the day of the
Lord is near—a day of clouds, a time of doom
for the nations.

Joel 1:15   Alas for that day! For the day of the
Lord is near; it will come like destruction from
the Almighty.

Joel 2:1–2   Let all who live in the land tremble,
for the day of the Lord is coming. It is close at
hand—a day of darkness and gloom, a day of
clouds and blackness. Like dawn spreading
across the mountains a large and mighty army
comes, such as never was of old nor ever will
be in ages to come.

Joel 2:11   The Lord thunders at the head of His
army; His forces are beyond number, and
mighty are those who obey His command. The
day of the Lord is great; it is dreadful. Who can
endure it?

Joel 2:31   The sun will be turned to darkness
and the moon to blood before the coming of the
great and dreadful day of the Lord.

Joel 3:14   Multitudes, multitudes in the valley of *decision*! For the day of the Lord is near in the valley of *decision*.

Amos 5:18–20   Woe to you who long for the day of the Lord! Why do you long for the day of the Lord? That day will be darkness, not light. It will be as though a man fled from a lion only to meet a bear, as though he entered his house and rested his hand on the wall only to have a snake bite him. Will not the day of the Lord be darkness, not light—pitch-dark, without a ray of brightness?

Obad. 15   The day of the Lord is near for all nations. As you have done, it will be done to you; your deeds will return upon your own head.

Zeph. 1:7   Be silent before the Sovereign Lord, for the day of the Lord is near. The Lord has prepared a sacrifice; He has consecrated those He has invited.

Zeph. 1:14   The great day of the Lord is near— near and coming quickly. Listen! The cry on the day of the Lord will be bitter, the shouting of the warrior there.

Zech. 14:1   A day of the Lord is coming when your plunder will be divided among you.

Mal. 4:5   See, I will send you the prophet Elijah before that great and dreadful day of the Lord comes.

Acts 2:20   The sun will be turned to darkness and the moon to blood before the coming of the great and glorious day of the Lord.

1 Cor. 5:5   Hand this man over to Satan, so that the sinful nature may be destroyed and his spirit saved on the day of the Lord.

1 Thess. 5:2   You know very well that the day of the Lord will come like a thief in the night.

2 Pet. 3:10   But the day of the Lord will come like a thief. The heavens will disappear with a roar; the elements will be destroyed by fire, and the earth and everything in it will be laid bare.

All of these statements have been quoted over and over to set the fear of God into people. But what these prophets were seeing was the human self's reaction to the end of its dominance, the End Times, and the beginning of the divine self's reign, forever and ever.

St. Paul's statement above is surprising (1 Cor.

5:5). He actually calls for one to be handed over to Satan for purging before the coming of the Lord. But if you recall, this is exactly the mission God gave Satan in the Book of Job.

> Job 1:8–12 Then the Lord said to Satan, "Have you considered my servant Job? There is no one on earth like him; he is blameless and upright, a man who fears God and shuns evil."
>
> "Does Job fear God for nothing?" Satan replied. "Have you not put a hedge around him and his household and everything he has? You have blessed the work of his hands, so that his flocks and herds are spread throughout the land. But stretch out your hand and strike everything he has, and he will surely curse you to your face."
>
> The Lord said to Satan, "Very well, then, everything he has is in your hands, but on the man himself do not lay a finger." Then Satan went out from the presence of the Lord.

In the ancient Hebrew teachings, Satan (literally, "adversary") is the accuser, as we see when he first speaks to God in Job, accusing Job of loving God only as long as his earthly self is satisfied. But he also becomes God's tester, putting Job to the test of his faith and patience.

Notice also how Satan first asks God to test Job's outer world, his possessions. When Job passes this test, then Satan seeks to test the inner world of Job's own being. The macro- and microcosms are important for us to understand.

Finally, in the New Testament, Satan becomes the tempter. As the Holy Spirit comes upon us (as it did Jesus), we will be led out into the desert to be tested, tempted and prepared for the coming of the Lord within ourselves and outside among others and the world—until, like Jesus, we can say, "Be gone, Satan, you have no part in me."[3]

THE SPIRITUALIZED "SON OF MAN" OR "MESSIAH" COMES

Daniel and the other prophets see the power of the heavens come upon these lower forces to judge and subdue or destroy them. Viewed from a microcosmic perspective, heaven in this context symbolizes our higher, godly selves coming more in control of our being and subduing these beastly forces. In the macrocosm, the great Spirit—God and Its forces—come and subdue these influences throughout the world.

Here are descriptions of the coming of the spirit:

Ezek. 1:25–2:2 Then there came a voice from above the expanse over [the beasts'] heads as they stood with lowered wings. [*The beasts are in a submissive pose, and the higher self is descending from the higher chakras to take command of the entire body temple.*]

Above the expanse over their heads was what looked like a throne of sapphire, and high above on the throne was a figure like that of a man. [*But this is the being with whom God originally shared the Garden.*]

I saw that from what appeared to be his waist up he looked like glowing metal, as if full of fire, and that from there down he looked like fire; and brilliant light surrounded him.

Like the appearance of a rainbow in the clouds on a rainy day, so was the radiance around him. This was the appearance of the likeness of the glory of the Lord. When I saw it, I fell facedown, and I heard the voice of one speaking.

He said to me, "Son of man, stand up on your feet and I will speak to you."

As he spoke, *the Spirit came into me* and raised me to my feet, and I heard him speaking to me.

Rev. 1:12–18   I turned around to see the voice that was speaking to me. And when I turned I saw seven golden lampstands, and among the lampstands was someone "like a son of man," dressed in a robe reaching down to his feet and with a golden sash around his chest.

His head and hair were white like wool, as white as snow, and his eyes were like blazing fire.

His feet were like bronze glowing in a furnace, and his voice was like the sound of rushing waters.

In his right hand he held seven stars, and out of his mouth came a sharp double-edged sword. His face was like the sun shining in all its brilliance.

When I saw him, I fell at his feet as though dead. Then he placed his right hand on me and said: "Do not be afraid. *I am the First and the Last. I am the Living One; I was dead, and behold I am alive for ever and ever!* And I hold the keys of death and Hades." [*This is the portion of us that died when we left the spiritual attunement for the earthly, physical life. Therefore, it was alive, was dead and behold is alive again.*]

Rev. 10:1   Then I saw another mighty angel coming down from heaven. He was robed in a cloud, with a rainbow above his head; his face was like the sun, and his legs were like fiery pillars.

Rev. 14:14   I looked, and there before me was a white cloud, and seated on the cloud was one "like a son of man" with a crown of gold on his head and a sharp sickle in his hand.

Each of these great visionaries saw the beastly urges of humanity make war with the heavenly forces of God and the godlings, but the heavenly forces ultimately win and rule forever. This occurs within each person. We each call forth our better selves, wrestle with our worst selves and, with the help of God, are ultimately victorious, becoming greater than even the angels for having been put to the test and the struggle and been found worthy.[4] As St. John says, "I, John, [am] your brother and companion in the suffering and kingdom and patient endurance that are ours in Jesus. . . ." (Rev. 1:9)

Of course, our primary interest in this book is the prophecies of the End Times in the outer world. However, it is important to keep in mind Hermes's great teaching, because the inner and outer cannot be totally isolated. Ultimately, they are one. But for our purposes here, we'll look at them separately.

CYCLES, RHYTHMS AND SOUL GROUPS

In order to fully understand how an ancient dream can have any bearing on our present time, we must understand the rhythms of life. Everything occurs in rhythms or cycles. When the mystery schools use the circle as the highest symbol of wisdom, it is because it is an emblem of the way life is. The ancient symbols of the circular serpent with its tail in its mouth and the goddess whose toes touch the top of her head to form a circle with her body are emblems of the circumferential movement or rhythm of life, in which the beginning is ultimately the ending.

Therefore, when the "son of man" in Daniel's dream interprets the horns as kingdoms, and then identifies the kingdoms as the Medes, the Persians and the Greeks, he is not simply speaking of their activities during Daniel's time, but a recurring cycle of these soul groups and their interaction with one another throughout the history of this realm. Their influence will return again and again, with different names, perhaps, but similar circumstances, until the End Times come. It is the way of things in this world—history repeats itself. Life pulsates. We move from activity to inactivity to activity again, from life to death to life again, from imagery to darkness to imagery again, from awake to sleep to awake again. Therefore, when the angel Gabriel says that Daniel's vision is a vision that "concerns the time of the end" and "the distant future," he is telling the truth.

To develop this idea of recurring cycles a little further, let's consider Daniel's dream of the outer world as we would an inner-world dream.

Media, Persia and Greece could be understood as symbols of different attitudes, urges and perspectives in life. In both his first and second visions, Daniel is told that the horns represent these three kingdoms and their wrestling with one another for power and influence. In one of Cayce's readings about the coming of the Messiah, he actually makes a reference to the ancient Persian king Xerxes! Why? What could ancient Xerxes have to do with the coming of the Messiah?

Xerxes was a powerful ruler of Persia who wanted to conquer the Greeks. Xerxes raised the largest army in history up until that time. But the way Xerxes got to Greece was through the aid of *the second church of John's Revelation,* Ephesus! Here's where Cayce's reference comes into play in our times. Cayce states it this way: ". . . when there is the turning back from the raising up of Xerxes as the deliverer from an unknown tongue or land, *and again is there seen that this occurs* in the entrance of the Messiah in this period." (1998) Clearly, Cayce is seeing the cycle coming around again; a cycle that began in ancient times. According to his view, the spiritual seekers looked to Xerxes (an earthly power) to deliver them from Greece's power and, in so doing, let his power take hold of them. It is trading one earthly master for another. Judas Iscariot looked to the man Jesus to deliver his people from the Romans with violence and power, but the man Jesus was looking to the spirit to deliver them all from the powers of the flesh and the world. As Jesus said to Peter when Peter wanted him to avoid his prophesied destiny, "Get behind me, Satan! You are a stumbling block to me; you do not have in mind the things of God, but the things of men." (Matt. 16:23)

When we turn away from seeking our deliverer in the flesh and instead seek him through our attunement to the spirit, then we see the Messiah's true influence. For our true liberation comes from the spirit, not the flesh. Remember, in Daniel's visions, the great beastly ruler was not overthrown "by human power."

Who or what influence and power is represented by Xerxes today? In what way is humanity still looking for its deliverance through earthly forces? Perhaps it is what the great Russian writer Leo Tolstoy foresaw on his deathbed—a vision of a great Antichrist coming in the future. It was a gigantic angel of darkness covering the whole earth, and across its chest was a banner that read, "Commercialism." We have seen four great powers attempt to take hold of the world in the 1900s: capitalism, fascism, communism and socialism. But none of these has been as powerfully captivating as the great force of *commercialism*. Every country has been affected by this force and its master, *materialism*. Most humans on earth are now bombarded with hypnotic persuasions to buy-buy, possess-possess, consume-consume. Once-sacred events are now brought to us by the grace and power of corporations whose primary goal is to sell product—for example, "the Olympics, brought to you by Coca-Cola and NBC." Tolstoy was shaken by what he saw, but he couldn't possibly have seen just how awesome this force would become across the world. The earth is covered with ads. All the great holy days are now commercialized holidays. The sacred images are replaced with the profane (e.g., the Easter bunny, Santa Claus). The birthday of the father of our country, George Washington, is now listed among the greatest shopping days. The ideals for which he struggled are lost in a buying spree.

Perhaps materialism, combined with commercialism, fits Daniel's vision that: "The fourth beast is a fourth kingdom that will appear on earth. It will be different from all the other kingdoms *and will devour the whole earth,* trampling it down and crushing it." No country or economic system is immune to the desires and lusts of its people. Eventually these forces will overwhelm the country. Seeing the material wealth of the

Western world and Japan, much of the rest of the world has lusted for their part in this. But they don't often see the dark side of materialism. Material wealth comes with a price. Usually that price is the suppression, or at least the limitation, of our spiritual nature and the accentuating of our lower nature.

One's attempts to awaken to the spirit, to seek the spirit's desires, to give birth to one's spiritual nature and attune to God, are now constantly challenged by the forces that demand material consumption, possession and gratification. Mammon is what it sells, and in order to keep selling, it must possess the consciousness of individuals, filling them with unending desire for more, more, more. But as the Master said, "No one can serve two masters. Either he will hate the one and love the other, or he will be devoted to the one and despise the other. You cannot serve both God and mammon." (Matt. 6:24)

True seekers of the spirit are constantly in a struggle with mammon's pull on them. In these excerpts from Psalm 73 the great seeker Asaph writes about his own struggle against envying the power of material possessions in this world. He almost lost his footing on the spiritual path because of it: "But I almost stumbled, my feet came close to slipping. For I was envious of the

arrogant. I saw their prosperity. They have increased in wealth. Surely in vain I have kept my
heart pure, and washed my hands in innocence.
When I pondered to understand this, it was
troublesome in my sight; until I came into the
sanctuary of God; then I perceived their end. As
for me, the nearness of God is my good."

The greatest beast to challenge the holy people
may well be materialism and its companion, commercialism. It breeds and supports desires for
outer-world things. It causes the children of God
to spend their resources of time, space and consciousness in the pursuit of more material gratification. On the Mount of Olives, Jesus warns that
in the latter days, powerful deceivers will come to
lead us off into outer pursuits, even *outer* pursuits
of God. Yet, the kingdom of God is *within* us. It is
spirit, not matter. It is life, not food. It is the beauty
of a loving heart and a smiling face, not clothing
and image. But the commercial forces would have
us believe that "image is everything"; material life
is "where it's at." They create a reality in which
contentment is found in consumption and possessions. Coke is "the real thing." They even take sacred
sayings and turn them around for the profane—
instead of "Jesus saves," we have "Datsun saves."

Jesus spent much of his time fighting these ideas:

Matt. 6:26 Consider the birds of the air; they
do not sow or reap or store away in barns, and

yet your heavenly Father feeds them. Are you not much more valuable than they?

Matt. 6:28–30   And why do you worry about clothes? See how the lilies of the field grow. They do not labor or spin. Yet I tell you, not even Solomon in all his splendor was dressed like one of these. If that is how God clothes the grass of the field, which is here today and tomorrow is thrown into the fire, will he not much more clothe you, O you of little faith?

Matt. 19:21   Jesus answered, "If you want to be perfect, go, sell your possessions and give to the poor, and you will have treasure in heaven. Then come, follow me."

Luke 12:33   Sell your possessions and give to the poor. Provide purses for yourselves that will not wear out, a treasure in heaven that will not be exhausted, where no thief comes near and no moth destroys.

In the Revelation, St. John sees the ultimate beast, and everyone who serves it must wear its mark upon them: "No one could buy or sell unless he had the mark, which is the name of the beast or the number of his name." (Rev. 13:17) Tolstoy may have seen the greatest beast to prevent the children of God from realizing their true potential.

For a balanced perspective on this issue, we need to also note that Jesus expressed a sense of decency and order in the material world by his teaching that we should "render unto Caesar that which is Caesar's and unto God that which is God's."[5] He, too, paid his taxes when the tax collector came[6]—revealing again his sense of co-operation and balance. What I believe he was teaching in the previously quoted passages is to "render unto God that which is God's." We tend to forget this part when we get into money, things and other earthly desires.

DANIEL'S SECOND VISION

Daniel's second vision in Daniel 8 is like the first, even though it occurred two years later. It contains three important changes that will indicate the End Times are at hand: 1) the daily sacrifice was ended, 2) no one was entering the sanctuary, and 3) the holy people were being trampled. This all leads to the "abomination of desolation" that Daniel sees and Jesus refers to in his talk on the Mount of Olives.

The Daily Sacrifice

The daily sacrifice refers to the offering up of outer self's interests for inner self's nourishment. This is done by setting aside time, space and consciousness for the spirit rather than the flesh. Few are doing this. It also refers to the sacrifice of self for another—getting out of one's self-centered world and caring about others. Jesus taught that no love is greater than that which sets aside one's interests for another's.[7] The Cayce readings say that Jesus' private prayer was, "Others, Lord, others." Rather than being consumed with our needs, we need to shift our consciousness and think of others' needs. This causes us to move out of individualness and more into universalness; to move from the little picture to the big picture. It expands us. I personally have found that when life is at its most dissatisfying, the best thing to do is look for someone who needs some help, and help them. It gets your mind off your problems, and before you know it, you feel better and your perspective seems clearer than before. It doesn't have to be something grand. Just helping someone move, fix something or make a connection can suffice. There's a magic in this that creates health—mental, emotional and physical health. Unfortunately, our culture attempts to solve dissatisfaction with food, appearance, medicine or even more focus on self! We need to remember the benefits of sacrifice, both for inner nourishment and physical health.

The Entering of the Sanctuary

The entering of the sanctuary refers to the movement of consciousness into the inner recesses of our being, where the spirit and kingdom of God abide. This is done through deep prayer, inner reflection, inner listening and meditation. There are examples of Jesus' practice of seeking time, space and consciousness so that he could enter the inner sanctuary:

Matt. 14:23 After he had dismissed them, he went up on a mountainside by himself to pray. When evening came, he was there alone.

Luke 6:12 One of those days Jesus went out to a mountainside to pray, and spent the night praying to God.

Matt. 26:36 Then Jesus went with his disciples to a place called Gethsemane, and he said to them, "Sit here while I go over there and pray."

Mark 1:35 Very early in the morning, while it was still dark, Jesus got up, left the house and went off to a solitary place, where he prayed.

The modern world doesn't set aside time, space and consciousness for attunement to the spirit. Religious services have become social engagements, outer greeting and talking events, not inner attunements. The sanctuary is within us. In order to get there, one has to go off to a quiet place and be still. As the psalm says: "Be still and know that I am God." (Ps. 46:10[8]) The Holy of Holies is left empty and unattended—both in the inner world of one's own microcosm and in the outer world of the macrocosm.

The Cayce readings say, "Mind and soul are the tabernacle." (1479-1) And in reading 2067-1, Cayce identifies the outer court of the temple as the body, the inner court as the mind, and the Holy of Holies as the spirit. Each person is the temple of the living God, lain out just as the outer temple.

Ezekiel receives this message in his vision when the Lord says, "Because you have defiled my sanctuary with all your vile images and detestable practices, I myself will withdraw. . . ." (Ezek. 5:11) This certainly sounds like the Lord is speaking of our inner sanctuary, where images abound.

The Trampling of the Holy People

The trampling of the holy people refers to the constant suppression of the influence of the God seekers by the forces that control the world. Spiritual pursuits are often suppressed by the forces of materialism, unless of course there's a commercial opportunity involved! Even religious television shows spend much of their time soliciting their viewers for more mammon, which in turn causes their viewers to go seek more mammon—and on and on it goes. "Trampling of the holy people" is also considered to be a reference to the attempted extermination of the Jews by the Nazis; an act that ultimately drove the Jews (whom Daniel would have considered to be "the holy people") to return to their homeland, restore their nation and become self-reliant again. All of which is foreshadowed in the prophecies of the End Times!

DANIEL'S THIRD VISION

Dan. 9:20–24   While I was speaking and praying, confessing my sin and the sin of my people Israel and making my request to the Lord my God for His holy hill—while I was still in prayer, Gabriel, the man I had seen in the earlier vision, came to me in swift flight about the time of the evening sacrifice.

He instructed me and said to me, *"Daniel, I have now come to give you insight and understanding.*

"As soon as you began to pray, an answer

was given, which I have come to tell you, for you are highly esteemed. Therefore, consider the message and understand the vision:

"Seventy 'sevens' are decreed for your people and your holy city to finish transgression, to put an end to sin, to atone for wickedness, to bring in everlasting righteousness, to seal up vision and prophecy and to anoint the most holy."

Well, here is the whole plan, clearly stated: The seekers ("your people") must: 1) finish with their self-seeking, 2) atone for their mistakes, 3) bring everlasting righteousness into their lives and the lives of those around them, and 4) anoint the Messiah—the Messiah *within* each of us and the Messiah *without* for the world. A set amount of time has been decreed for this to happen: seventy cycles of sevens.

It continues:

Dan. 9:25–27 "Know and understand this: *From the issuing of the decree to restore and rebuild Jerusalem until the Messiah, the ruler, comes, there will be seven 'sevens,' and sixty-two 'sevens.'* It will be rebuilt with streets and a trench, but in times of trouble.

"After the sixty-two 'sevens,' the Messiah will be cut off and will have nothing. The people of the ruler who will come will destroy the city and the sanctuary. The end will come like a flood: War will continue until the end, and desolations have been decreed.

"He [*the earthly ruler who will come*] will confirm a covenant with many for one 'seven.' In the middle of the 'seven' he will put an end to sacrifice and offering. And on a wing [*of the temple*] he will set up *an abomination that causes desolation*, until the end that is decreed is poured out on him."

Since the rebuilding of the temple and the coming of the Messiah is a recurring theme, we need to understand this better. In attempting to understand the phrase: "From the issuing of the decree to restore and rebuild Jerusalem until the Messiah comes, there will be seven 'sevens,'" we need a little history lesson.

The temple in Jerusalem was first built by Solomon "in the four hundred and eightieth year after the people of Israel came out of the land of Egypt, in the fourth year of Solomon's reign over Israel, in the month of Ziv." This would be April–May of approximately 1440 B.C., though most scholars prefer 960 B.C.[9] This great temple was destroyed in 587–586 B.C. by the Babylonians.[10] It was rebuilt in the second year of Darius I, 520 B.C.,[11] and destroyed again by Titus in A.D. 70. It has not been rebuilt. Upon its site is now the Islamic mosque Dome of the Rock.

Daniel's visions occurred in the years 554, 552

and 535 B.C. Clearly the temple and Jerusalem were rebuilt *after* Daniel's visions, in 520 B.C., and then destroyed again in A.D. 70. There appears to be a cycle here. Built in 960, destroyed in 586, rebuilt in 520, destroyed in 70. Since Gabriel said that the vision was of the distant future and the times of the end, we can assume the temple will be rebuilt again.

The Edgar Cayce readings teach that the vision of Daniel, especially chapter 12, refers to World War II. Cayce also said that one of the purposes of World War II was to begin the return of the Jews to Israel in 1947. So we can assume that the phrase, "from the issuing of the decree to rebuild and restore Jerusalem until the Messiah comes, there will be seven 'sevens,' " might well be speaking of this period. If 1947 is the year of the decree to restore Israel's Jerusalem, then adding forty-nine years (i.e., "seven 'sevens' ") to 1947 would mean that 1996 is the year of the coming of the Messiah. The Cayce readings say 1998. Nostradamus implies 1999. The Holy Mother seems to be indicating that it coincides with the end of the line of popes, which she says ends with this current pope, Pope John Paul II. So I think we can say that there is prophetic agreement that the coming of the Messiah may occur somewhere between 1996 and 1999. Of course, many have tried to figure this out before us, and have come up with different ideas, but there is supporting evidence for this time frame: 1996 to 1999.

If we consider what this means within ourselves, then from the time that we issue the decree to rebuild our holy consciousness and the temples of our bodies for the abiding of our godly selves, it will take seven seven-year cycles until the Messiah comes within us. This idea fits very well with Cayce's teachings that the body completely rebuilds itself every seven years and that we will indeed have new bodies during the period when the Messiah reigns for a thousand years of peace. Cayce references St. Paul's comments on this:

> 1 Cor. 15:51–52 Listen, I tell you a mystery:
> We will not all sleep, but we will all be
> changed—in a flash, in the twinkling of an eye,
> at the last trumpet. For the trumpet will sound,
> the dead will be raised imperishable, and we
> will be changed.

In Cayce's comments about a "new root race," he explains that the human race is on the verge of another major change in its body structure. He says that what St. Paul is referring to is just that, a new body. The body structure that we currently inhabit is approximately forty thousand years old. In other words, scientists can find remains dating as far back as forty thousand years ago that match our present bodies. Beyond that time period, all humanoid remains are different from our present structure. Is it a coincidence that forty is once again the unit involved here? Recall Noah's forty days and nights, Israel's forty years in the desert, Moses' staying on the mountain with God for forty days and nights, Jesus' forty days and nights in the desert, and our bodies being forty thousand years old. Perhaps a change is about to happen, because the cycle has come around to the appropriate moment.

What then is meant by the phrase, "after sixty-two 'sevens' the Messiah will be cut off and will have nothing"? Then it goes on to say that the people and the ruler who is to come will put an end to the city and sanctuary (i.e., Jerusalem and the temple), and will put an end to sacrifice and offering, and will set up an abomination that causes desolation. This will happen until the End Times come upon this ruler and his people. What does this mean?

The Christian answer is that the Israelites' John the Baptist and Jesus of Nazareth were the prophesied return of Elijah and the Messiah, respectively, and that the Messiah reigned for a time and then was cut off. His temple (body) was destroyed, but resurrected, and ultimately the outer temple was destroyed in A.D. 70. The Israelites were then scattered throughout the earth, until the time of the end drew near—when they would be called back to restore and rebuild Jerusalem and the temple. In the meantime, "the people and their ruler" were the Gentiles and the spirit of materialism and earthly power that has reigned for these past two thousand years. But the age of the Gentiles is coming to an end, and the Messiah will return with power, and all will be changed.

ARMAGEDDON

The only biblical passage to use this name is in the Book of the Revelation. Here are the relevant verses:

Rev. 16:13–19 Then I saw three evil spirits that looked like frogs; they came out of the mouth of the dragon, out of the mouth of the beast and out of the mouth of the false prophet. They are spirits of demons performing miraculous signs, and they go out to the kings of the whole world, to gather them for the battle on the great day of God Almighty. "Behold, I come like a thief! Blessed is he who stays awake and keeps his clothes with him, so that he may not go naked and be shamefully exposed." Then they gathered the kings together to the place that in Hebrew is called *Armageddon*. The seventh angel poured out his bowl into the air, and out of the temple came a loud voice from the throne, saying, "It is done!" Then there came flashes of lightning, rumblings, peals of thunder and a severe earthquake. No earthquake like it has ever occurred since man has been on earth, so tremendous was the quake. The great city split into three parts, and the cities of the nations collapsed. God remembered Babylon the Great and gave her the cup filled with the wine of the fury of his wrath.

Notice how this event is marked by a severe earth change, an earthquake like none other man has seen on earth! Armageddon literally means "Hill of Megiddo," the site of several decisive battles in Israel's history (see Judg. 5:19, 2 Kings 9:27 and 2 Chron. 35:22). The reference to the "great city" is believed by many to be Rome, a city the disciple John would have considered to be a great earthly power at his time. Babylon the Great would be symbolic of materiality and commercialism, the enemy of spirituality and community. Changes in Rome are also seen by Nostradamus and Mother Mary as a key sign of the coming of the End Times.

At this point, let's read what Jesus says on the Mount of Olives.

Jesus' Teaching on the Mount of Olives

Matt. 24:1–3 Jesus left the temple and was walking away when His disciples came up to Him to call His attention to its buildings. [*This would have been about A.D. 70.*]

"Do you see all these things?" He asked. "I tell you the truth, not one stone here will be left on another; every one will be thrown down." [*The temple was destroyed in A.D. 70.*]

As Jesus was sitting on the Mount of Olives, the disciples came to Him privately. "Tell us," they said, *"when will this happen, and what will be the sign of your coming and of the end of the age?"*

Our earthly selves naturally tend to understand time and prophecy from a *linear* perspective—first this will happen, then this and finally that. However, our higher selves and the spiritual realm see time and prophecy from a holistic perspective—this has, is, and will happen again and again until the rhythm, the pulse, the cycle is complete. Therefore a great visionary can be speaking of a distant future as well as an imminent present. So when Jesus answers what appears to us to be a question about the immediate future, he may actually be giving a more holistic answer. And later, when he says, "I tell you the truth, this generation will certainly not pass away until all these things have happened," he may be correct, even though all these disciples died before the End Times. Those listening to him will experience every bit of it within their microcosms, and ultimately within the macrocosm. Remember, all the dead will be called to life again.[12] The Mount of Olives teaching continues:

Matt. 24:4–8 Jesus answered: "Watch out that no one deceives you.

"For many will come in my name, claiming, 'I am the Messiah,'[13] and will deceive many.

"You will hear of wars and rumors of wars, but see to it that you are not alarmed. Such things must happen, but the end is still to come.

"Nation will rise against nation, and kingdom against kingdom. There will be famines and earthquakes in various places.

"All these are the beginning of birth pains."

See how Jesus uses this metaphor to explain the suffering and changes that must come about? The End Times are the birth of the spirit. Like a woman in labor, we will suffer pain in our attempts to deliver our spiritual selves. The teaching continues:

> Matt. 24:9–11 "Then you will be handed over to be persecuted and put to death, and you will be hated by all nations because of me.
>
> "At that time *many will turn away from the faith* and will betray and hate each other, and *many false prophets will appear and deceive many people.*"

In the 1900s we have seen the falling away from the faith. Who can forget *The New York Times*'s headline: "God is dead!" And false prophets have become so common that many deceived seekers have already been deprogrammed! But the seekers keep coming. Some in the guise of religious leaders, some as political leaders, some as psychological liberators. Another amazing phenomenon has been the paganizing of the country that was founded with the slogan "In God We Trust" printed on its money. The freedom this country provided the world has been used against it to undermine its values and purposes. Now, instead of a healthy separation of church and state, we have a state that can have no semblance of trusting in or calling upon God.

The Mount of Olives teaching continues:

Matt. 9:12–13   "Because of the increase of law-lessness, the love of most will grow cold, but he who stands firm to the end will be saved."

If there is one prophecy that I feel we all can point to for evidence that we are in the latter days, it is this one. From Asia, through the United States and Europe and on into Russia, the Middle East and India, lawlessness has taken a hold on daily life that has not been seen be-fore. Crime is everywhere. Some countries are actually ruled by criminal forces. Many fear that the newly dissolved Soviet Union has left Russia a lawless country run by the forces of the underworld.

The Mount of Olives teaching continues:

Matt. 9:14   "And this gospel of the kingdom will be preached in the whole world as a testi-mony to all nations, and then *the end will come*."

Most Christians point to this prophecy as a sign that we are near to the end. The gospel of "love God with all thy being, and thy neighbor as thyself" has now been preached across the world. In the year 2000, Christianity was the re-ligion of 31.2 percent of the world's popula-tion—the largest religion, with adherents in every country.

The prophecy continues:

Matt. 9:15–33 *"So when you see standing in the holy place the abomination that causes desolation, spoken of through the prophet Daniel—let the reader understand*—then let those who are in Judea flee to the mountains.

"Let no one on the roof of his house go down to take anything out of the house.

"Let no one in the field go back to get his cloak.

"How dreadful it will be in those days for pregnant women and nursing mothers!

"Pray that your flight will not take place in winter or on the Sabbath.

"For then there will be great distress, unequaled from the beginning of the world until now—and never to be equaled again.

"If those days had not been cut short, no one would survive, but for the sake of the elect those days will be shortened.

"At that time if anyone says to you, 'Look, here is the Messiah!' or, 'There he is!' do not believe it.

"For false Messiahs and false prophets will appear and perform great signs and miracles to deceive even the elect—if that were possible.

"See, I have told you ahead of time.

"So if anyone tells you, 'There he is, out in the desert,' do not go out; or, 'Here he is, in the inner rooms,' do not believe it.

"For as lightning that comes from the east is visi-

*ble even in the west, so will be the coming of the
Son of Man.*

"Wherever there is a carcass, there the vul-
tures will gather.

"Immediately after the distress of those days
the sun will be darkened, and the moon will
not give its light; the stars will fall from the sky,
and the heavenly bodies will be shaken.

"At that time the sign of the Son of Man will
appear in the sky, and all the nations of the
earth will mourn. They will see the Son of Man
coming on the clouds of the sky, with power
and great glory.

"And he will send his angels with a loud trum-
pet call, and they will gather his elect from the four
winds, from one end of the heavens to the other.

"Now learn this lesson from the fig tree: As
soon as its twigs get tender and its leaves come
out, you know that summer is near.

*"Even so, when you see all these things, you know
that it is near, right at the door."*

Jesus may be referring to the door of our con-
sciousnesses, as well as the door into this world.

Matt. 9:34–35 "I tell you the truth, this generation will certainly not pass away until all these
things have happened.

*"Heaven and earth will pass away, but my words
[logos] will never pass away."*

Jesus is using the Greek word *logos* instead of *lalia* for "word." Logos means more than "word." It means the central essence of being.

> Matt. 9:36–39 "No one knows about that day or hour, not even the angels in heaven, nor the Son, but only the Father.
> *"As it was in the days of Noah, so it will be at the coming of the Son of Man."*
> "For in the days before the flood, people were eating and drinking, marrying and giving in marriage, up to the day Noah entered the ark; and they understood nothing about what would happen until the flood came and took them all away. *That is how it will be at the coming of the Son of Man."*

There are several indications that Jesus is speaking about the inner and outer worlds and forces. The dire descriptions make it sound impossible to live through this coming birth: "There will be great distress, unequaled from the beginning of the world until now—and never to be equaled again." And, "If those days had not been cut short, no one would survive, but for the sake of the elect those days will be shortened." If you've ever watched a woman give birth, then you know how impossible it all seems. When asked how any can be saved, Jesus answered, "With man it is impossible, but with God all things are possible."

Individuals and the world may seem to be dying in a whirl of fire and flood, but the spark of the spirit within each soul and in the world will be delivered and reign for ever and ever. We will not die, but all will be changed.

Rev. 21:1–6 *Then I saw a new heaven and a new earth, for the first heaven and the first earth had passed away, and there was no longer any sea.*

I saw the Holy City, the new Jerusalem, coming down out of heaven from God, prepared as a bride beautifully dressed for her husband.

And I heard a loud voice from the throne saying, *"Now the dwelling of God is with men, and He will live with them. They will be His people, and God Himself will be with them and be their God.*

"He will wipe every tear from their eyes. There will be no more death or mourning or crying or pain, for the old order of things has passed away."

He who was seated on the throne said, "I am making everything new!" Then he said, "Write this down, for these words are trustworthy and true."

He said to me: "It is done. I am the Alpha and the Omega, *the Beginning and the End.* To him who is thirsty I will give to drink freely from the spring of the Water of Life."

Certainly, the End Times prophecies in the

Bible are something to be seriously considered. They include a war greater than any yet fought on earth, an earthquake larger than any experienced on earth and many other serious challenges to physical life as we know it. However, woven through all these terrible events is a thread of light that leads us to "the glory that was ours before the world was."

2

THE PROPHECIES OF
EDGAR CAYCE

From the mid 1920s to 1944, Edgar Cayce produced more material on the End Times and earth changes than any other source I know of. The volume of material is staggering. More important, much of the material is very specific to what will happen and when.

Edgar Cayce (pronounced KAY-see) was born on a farm near Hopkinsville, Kentucky, on 18 March 1877. As a child, he displayed unusual powers of perception. At the age of six, he told his parents that he could see and talk with "visions," sometimes of relatives who had recently died, and even with angels. He could also sleep with his head on his schoolbooks and awake with a photographic recall of their contents, even citing the page upon which specific information appeared. However, after completing seventh grade, he left school—which was not unusual for boys at that time.

When he was twenty-one, he developed a paralysis of the throat muscles that caused him to lose his voice. When doctors were unable to find a physical cause for this condition, Edgar Cayce asked a friend to help him reenter the same kind of hypnotic sleep that had enabled him to memorize his schoolbooks as a child. The friend gave him the necessary suggestions, and once he was in this trance state, Cayce spoke clearly and directly without any difficulty. He instructed the hypnotist to give him a suggestion to increase the blood flow to his throat; when the suggestion was given, Cayce's throat turned bloodred. Still under hypnosis, Cayce recommended some specific medication and manipulative therapy that would aid in restoring his voice completely.

On subsequent occasions, Cayce would go into the hypnotic state to diagnose and prescribe healing for others, with much success. Doctors around Hopkinsville and Bowling Green, Kentucky, took advantage of Cayce's unique talent to diagnose their patients. They soon discovered that all Cayce needed was the name and address of a patient to "tune in" telepathically to that individual's mind and body. The patient didn't have to be near Cayce; he could tune in to them wherever they were.

When one of the young MDs working with Cayce submitted a report on his strange abilities to a clinical research society in Boston, the reactions were amazing. On 9 October 1910, *The New York Times* carried two pages of headlines and pictures. From then on, people from all over the country sought the "sleeping prophet," as he was to become known.

The routine he used for conducting a trance diagnosis was to recline on a couch, his hands folded across his solar plexus, and breathe deeply. Eventually his eyelids would begin fluttering and his breathing would become deep and rhythmical. This was the signal to the conductor (usually his wife, Gertrude) to make verbal contact with Cayce's subconscious by giving a suggestion. Unless this suggestion was timed to synchronize with his fluttering eyelids and the change in his breathing, Cayce would continue beyond his trance state and simply fall fast asleep. However, if the suggestion was made in time, Cayce would proceed to describe the patient as though he or she were sitting right next to him, his mind functioning much as an X-ray scanner, seeing into every organ of the patient's body. When he was finished, he would say,

"Ready for questions." However, in many cases his mind would have already anticipated the patient's questions, answering them during the main session. Finally, he would say, "We are through for the present," whereupon the conductor would give the suggestion to return to normal consciousness.

If this procedure were in any way violated, Cayce would be in serious personal danger. On one occasion, he remained in a trance state for three days and had actually been given up for dead by the attending doctors.

At each session, a stenographer (usually Gladys Davis Turner, his personal secretary) would record everything Cayce said. Sometimes, during a trance session, Cayce would even correct the stenographer's spelling. It was as though his mind were in touch with everything around him and beyond.

Each client was identified with a number to keep their names private. For example, hypnotic material for Edgar Cayce is filed under the number 294. His first "reading," as they were called, would be numbered 294-1, and each subsequent reading would increase the dash number (294-2, 294-3 and so on). Some numbers refer to groups of people, such as 262 for the Study Group, and some numbers refer to specific research or guidance readings, such as the 254 series containing the Work readings dealing with the overall work of the organization that grew up around him, and the 364 and 996 series containing the readings on Atlantis.

It was 10 August 1923 before anyone thought to ask the "sleeping" Cayce for insights beyond physical health—questions about life, death and human destiny. In a small hotel room in Dayton, Ohio, Arthur Lammers asked the first set of philosophical questions that were to lead to an entirely new way of using Cayce's strange abilities. It was during this line of questioning that Cayce first began to talk about reincarnation as though it were as real and natural as the functionings of a physical body. This shocked and challenged Cayce and his family. They were deeply religious people, doing this work to help others because that's what their Christian faith taught. Reincarnation was not part of their reality. Yet the healings and help continued to come. So the Cayce family continued with the physical material, but cautiously reflected on the strange philosophical material. Ultimately the Cayces began to accept the ideas, though not as "reincarnation" per se. Edgar Cayce preferred to call it the "Continuity of Life." As a child, he read the Bible from front to back, and did so for every year of his life. He felt that it contained much evidence that life, the true life in the spirit, is continual.

Eventually Edgar Cayce, following advice from his own readings, moved to Virginia Beach, Virginia, and set up a hospital where he continued to conduct his physical readings for the health of others. But he also continued this new line of readings called life readings. From 1925 to 1944, he conducted some twenty-five hundred of these life readings, describing the past lives of individuals as casually as if everyone understood reincarnation were a reality. Such subjects as deep-seated fears, mental blocks, vocational talents, innate urges and abilities, marriage difficulties, child training and so forth were examined in the light of what the readings called the "karmic patterns" resulting from previous lives spent by the individual's soul on the earth plane.

When he died on 3 January 1945 in Virginia Beach, Cayce left well over fourteen thousand documented stenographic records of the telepathic-clairvoyant readings he had given for more than six thousand different people over a period of forty-three years.

The readings constitute one of the largest and most impressive records of psychic perception. Together with their relevant records, correspondence and reports, they have been cross-indexed under thousands of subject headings and placed at the disposal of doctors, psychologists, students, writers and investigators, who still come to examine them. They are also available to the general public in topical books on or complete volumes of the readings, as well as on CD-ROM.

A foundation known as the Association for Research and Enlightenment (A.R.E.) was founded in 1932 to preserve these readings. An open-membership research society, it continues to index and catalog the readings, initiate investigation and experiments, and conduct conferences, seminars and lectures. The A.R.E. also has the largest and finest library of parapsychological and metaphysical books in the world.[1]

THE PROBLEM WITH INTERPRETING HIS READINGS

Edgar Cayce's readings do present some difficulties in interpretation and understanding. First, they are somewhat hard to read, mostly due to their syntax and the presence of archaic or biblical terms and style. They are *written* records of *oral* presentations, which occasionally do not carry the full intent that was expressed; even punctuation can significantly change the meaning or intent of the voiced statement. Also, most of the readings were given to specific people with personal perspectives and prejudices on the topics being discussed, and therefore the responses were unique to each seeker. For example, in a reading for one person Cayce recommends one marriage for life, to another he recommends never getting married and to a third he encourages him to marry at least twice. In the few cases where a reading was purposefully done for a broader presentation to many people, the "sleeping" Cayce was still somewhat at the mercy and wisdom of those directing the session and asking the questions. Nevertheless, Cayce and his wife, Gertrude, and their assistant, Gladys, were very conscientious people, always seeking to be exact and true to the original intent of the reading. As I indicated earlier, the "sleeping" Cayce would occasionally stop his direct discourse to give an aside to Gladys about the way she was recording the material, correcting spelling or giving a clarifying explanation of something he had just said.

Finally, the paragraphs are so complex because some of Cayce's readings cover so many points or issues, and it can be difficult to determine which issue he is referring to. Despite all this, with practice, one can become familiar enough with the syntax, terms and *thys, thees* and *thous*; the repetitive use of the word *that*; and the complex thought pattern that one can learn to read and understand the Cayce readings fairly easily. Still, experienced readers of Cayce's work can examine the same readings and come up with differing views as to what they mean.

For example, on the topic of End Times and earth changes, there are differing views within A.R.E. as to just what is going to happen, if anything. Some believe that the Cayce readings have predicted earth changes that simply have not occurred. In other words, he was wrong, and could therefore be wrong about everything. Others say that these readings were misinterpreted, and the changes spoken of are yet to come. Some claim that there are Cayce readings that say the earth changes are all subject to modification or even suspension of their prophesied outcome if humanity makes certain changes in their hearts and minds. Others believe Cayce's readings state that some earth changes are virtual actualities waiting for their time to manifest—simply a matter of destiny. The sheer volume and complexity of the material makes it difficult for everyone to agree on what is in the readings and what they mean. I hope I can clarify some of this for all our sakes.

Most of the Cayce readings presented in this book are edited for clarity, readability and their focus on the point at hand. However, I've included all the reading numbers so you can review the originals, if you wish. When Cayce was engaged with a specific person in a mind-to-mind discussion or even a debate about these issues, I have attempted to show the whole of that discussion/debate, even when it covers several issues beyond the End Times and earth changes. I believe this gives us a better understanding of the overall context of the reading.

During the Great Depression, Cayce lost the magnificent building on the hill overlooking the ocean in Virginia Beach, Virginia, that was the home to his work. It depressed him so much that some were concerned about the quality of his readings during this time. This is particularly true of the earth-change readings given through the "sleeping" Cayce that included an entity called "Halaliel." I have deliberately kept these readings separate. In this way I can show how Cayce continued to give similar earth-change readings long after Halaliel was gone. Nevertheless, the Halaliel readings have some of the most interesting perspectives on these prophecies of change. Therefore, let's begin with them.

PROPHECIES CONVEYED THROUGH CAYCE BY HALALIEL

Halaliel (pronounced Ha-la-lee-EL) first identified himself through the "sleeping" Cayce on

15 October 1933 during a Study Group reading on the lesson titled "Day and Night." There had been fifty-five readings given to this Study Group. Occasionally messages had come through the "sleeping" Cayce from other entities in the spirit realms, but never was the complete reading credited to a single spirit entity. The reading began and continued as usual, but it ended on a strange note. Here is the last question of this reading and the answer given.

Q: *Comment upon the following. Does it carry any light of truth?*

The Creator, in seeking to create a being worthy of companionship, realized that such a being would result only from having free will and exercising its divine inheritance through its own efforts to find its Maker. Thus, making the choice really a Divine one has caused the existence of states of consciousness, that would indeed tax the free will of a soul; thus light and darkness. Truly, only those tried "so as by fire" can enter in.

A: The only variation that we would make is that all souls in the beginning were *one* with the Father. The separation, or turning away, brought evil. Then there became the necessity of the awareness of self's being out of accord with blessedness, or out of the realm of blessedness; and, as given of the Son, "yet learned he obedience through the things which he suffered."

COME, my children! Ye no doubt have

gained from the comment this day, *a new initiate has spoken in or through this channel; Halaliel, that was with those in the beginning who warred with those that separated themselves and became as naught.* [my italics] (262-56)

The closing line refers to the legendary battle between the angels of rebellion, led by Lucifer, and the angels of light, led by Michael. Apparently Halaliel was among those angels of light that warred with the separating angels, who later became known as the Fallen Angels.

The next time Halaliel is mentioned by the "sleeping" Cayce is on 24 October 1933 at a morning reading. This time the reading is a research reading dealing with the subjects of psychic phenomena, spiritism and spiritualism. The reading ends very strangely again, giving a list of entities who can be of help in gaining a better understanding of these concepts and instructing the conductor (Gertrude Cayce, Edgar's wife) to call these "forces" to be present for the next reading.

The forces gathered here may be used in gaining this concept. As ye seek, ask first if all these are present: Lamech, Confucius, Tamah, Halaliel, Hebe, Ra, Ra-Ta, John. (5756-10)

That very afternoon, at the 3:00 P.M. reading, Gertrude began the reading in accord with the morning suggestion.

GC [*Gertrude Cayce*]: If the "forces" Lamech, Confucius, Tamah, Halaliel, Hebe, Ra, Ra-Ta, John are present, we seek the answer to the following question. (5756-11)

Gladys's notes at the end of this reading include this statement: "Edgar Cayce said on waking that he would like to always feel surrounded by as helpful influences as he did this time."

On 7 January 1934, the fifty-seventh Study Group reading was given, and one of those in attendance asked, "Who is Halaliel?" Here's the answer:

One in and with whose courts Ariel fought when there was the rebellion in heaven. Now, where is heaven? Where is Ariel, and who was he? A companion of Lucifer or Satan, and one that made for the disputing of the influences in the experiences of Adam in the Garden. (262-57)

Clearly we are dealing with the legendary war of the angels. All the angels were originally created in the image of the Creator, but through the misuse of free will, some rebelled against the cooperative spirit of oneness. This rebellion would not be allowed; it was like a cancer in the universal consciousness. So they were driven from heaven until such time that they repented of their self-seeking ways and reattuned themselves to the Creator's harmonious spirit of oneness. Notice that the literal meanings of their names are quite beautiful and powerful, as they were originally intended to be: *Ariel* means "lion of God" and *Lucifer* means "light giver." The name Satan is actually from a Hebrew word that simply means "adversary." This is why the Messiah is often called the "advocate"; he is our counterinfluence to the adversary.

At the end of this reading, Gladys noted that Edgar Cayce had a slightly different experience during the reading. Normally he would go to the Hall of Records to receive the Book of Life (the records) of the individual for whom the reading was being given. This time he felt that a "group activity" took place in the back of the building where he received the records. Could this have been the group of Lamech, Confucius, Tamah, Halaliel, Hebe, Ra, Ra-Ta and John?

The very next time Halaliel is mentioned is on 8 January 1934 in a reading for a female society leader and Theosophist, subject 443. She had been asking a series of very involved questions about mysticism and spiritual truth, then she asked:

Q: *How high is the source that this information is being given from?*

A: From the universal forces, and as emanated through the teacher that gives same—as one that has been given—Halaliel. (443-3)

A few days later, on the nineteenth, we get the first earth changes material of which at least some portion of the reading was delivered by Halaliel, because he says so in the midst of the reading. This whole reading is unusual. For the first time the Cayces use a recording instrument to record the reading. Instead of Gertrude conducting, their eldest son, Hugh Lynn Cayce, is the conductor, and in his opening suggestion to Edgar, he instructs Edgar to stop every fifteen minutes so the recording device can be reloaded. Amazingly, the "sleeping" Edgar stops exactly every fifteen minutes throughout the reading, even if he is in midsentence. Here is Hugh Lynn's opening suggestion and the "sleeping" Edgar's response:

Q: *We seek at this time such information as will be of value and interest to those present regarding the spiritual, mental and physical changes which are coming to the earth. You will tell us what part we may play in meeting and helping others to understand these changes. At the end of each fifteen-minute period you will pause, until I tell you to*

*continue, while the recording instrument is being
arranged. You will speak distinctly at a normal
rate of speech, and you will answer the questions
which we ask.*

A: Yes; as each of you gathered here have
your own individual development, yet as each
seeks to be a channel of blessings to the fellow
man, each attunes self to the Throne of universal information. And, there may be accorded
you that which may be beneficial, not only in
thine own experience, but that which will prove
helpful, hopeful, in the experience of others.
(3976-15)

From here, the reading goes into a brief description of the number and nature of the spirit
entities that are gathered about them now to
help with this reading. Then the reading tells of
the return of one of their members to the earth
to help with this coming period of earth changes.
The returning entity is the disciple John the Beloved. Then the reading begins to address the
coming earth changes. Remember, the reading
is being given in January 1934.

As to the material changes that are to be as an
omen, as a sign to those that this is shortly to
come to pass—as has been given of old, the
sun will be darkened and the earth shall be
broken up in divers places[2]—and THEN shall

be PROCLAIMED—through the spiritual in-
terception in the hearts and minds and souls
of those that have sought His way—that HIS
star has appeared, and will point the way for
those that enter into the holy of holies in themselves. For, God the Father, God the Teacher,
God the director, in the minds and hearts of
men, must ever be IN those that come to know
Him as first and foremost in the seeking of
those souls; for He is first the GOD to the individual and as He is exemplified, as He is manifested in the heart and in the acts of the body
of the individual, then He becomes manifested
before men. And those that seek in the latter
portion of the year of our Lord (as ye have
counted in and among men) '36, He will appear. (3976-15)

My italics isolate the phrase that fits so well
with the Daniel visions. Recall that one of Daniel's visions was of entering the sanctuary, the
holy of holies within each of us. Here Halaliel
speaks to the same activity, saying that those
who do go within their sanctuary will know,
will be guided. The "He will appear" idea is
further developed elsewhere in the Cayce readings. Cayce says that the Messiah first comes
in the hearts and minds of those that seek this
influence, then it moves into the physical realm,
ultimately becoming fully manifest, as we are,

and incarnate. Cayce says, "He will walk and talk with people of every clime." (364-13) Halaliel states here that the beginning of this process is in 1936, for those that seek within themselves. Then Halaliel continues, focusing on earth changes. These are shifts and disruptions in the earth that have been associated with the Cayce readings, particularly of late:

As to the changes physical again: The earth will be broken up in the western portion of America. The greater portion of Japan must go into the sea. The upper portion of Europe will be changed as in the twinkling of an eye. Land will appear off the east coast of America. There will be the upheavals in the Arctic and in the Antarctic that will make for the eruption of volcanoes in the Torrid areas [*the area between the Tropic of Cancer and the Tropic of Capricorn*], and there will be shifting then of the poles—so that where there has been those of a frigid or the semitropical will become the more tropical, and moss and fern will grow. And these will *begin* in those periods in '58 to '98, when these will be proclaimed as the periods when His light will be seen again in the clouds. As to times, as to seasons, as to places, ALONE is it given to those who have named the name—and who bear the mark of those of His calling and His election in their bodies. To them it shall be given.

As to those things that deal with the mental of the earth, these shall call upon the mountains to cover many. As ye have seen those in lowly places raised to those of power in the political, in the machinery of nations' activities, so shall ye see those in high places reduced and calling on the waters of darkness to cover them. And those that in the inmost recesses of their selves awaken to the spiritual truths that are to be given, and those places that have acted in the capacity of teachers among men, the rottenness of those that have ministered in places will be brought to light, and turmoils and strifes shall enter. And, as there is the wavering of those that would enter as emissaries, as teachers, from the throne of life, the throne of light, the throne of immortality, and wage war in the air with those of darkness, then know ye the Armageddon is at hand. For with the great numbers of the gathering of the hosts of those that have hindered and would make stumbling blocks for man and his weaknesses, they shall wage war with the spirits of light that come into the earth for this awakening; that have been and are being called by those of the sons of men into the service of the living God. For He, as ye have been told, is not the God of the dead, not the God of those that have forsaken Him, but those that love His coming, that love His associations among men—the God of the LIVING, the God of Life! For, He IS Life. (3976-15)

At this point, the reading shifts back to the return of John the Beloved, whose name is stated as John Peniel (pronounced pen-ee-EL). *Peniel* means "face of God" in Hebrew, and was the name Jacob gave to the place where he met God face-to-face and where his own name was changed to Israel, which means "strives with God." The reading says that John will be known in America by those that have gone through the regeneration in their bodies, minds and spirits, and that he will give "the new order of things." John will be able to make these things "PLAIN in the minds of men, that they may know the truth, the life, the light, will make them free."

Then the reading goes into an intense, inspiring call to awaken, filled with biblical phrases and ending with Halaliel identifying himself as the deliverer of this information:

I have declared this, that has been delivered unto me to give unto you, ye that sit here and that hear and that see a light breaking in the east, and have heard, have seen thine weaknesses and thine faultfindings, and know that He will make thy paths straight if ye will but live that YE KNOW this day. Then, may the next step, the next word, be declared unto thee. For ye in your weakness have known the way, through that as ye have made manifest of the

SPIRIT of truth and light that has been proclaimed into this earth, that has been committed
unto the keeping of Him that made of Himself
no estate but who brought into being all that
ye see manifest in the earth. He has declared
this message unto thee: "Love the Lord thy God
with all thine heart," and the second is like unto
it, "Love thy neighbor as thyself." Who is thine
neighbor? Him that ye may aid in whatsoever
way that he, thy neighbor, thy brother, has been
troubled. Help him to stand on his own feet.
For such may only know the acceptable way.
The weakling, the unsteady, must enter into the
crucible and become as naught, even as He, that
they may know the way. I, Halaliel, have spoken. (3976-15)

This is followed by a series of questions from
the participants. The first question deals directly
with the earth changes, and it is here that Halaliel begins to get into trouble with future students of this material. They point out that the
first question asks what earth changes would
occur "this year"; that would have been 1934.
But the answer clearly does not address 1934,
nor did any of the changes mentioned occur in
1934. Perhaps Halaliel's consciousness was too
vast to focus on 1934, or 1934 never made a
sufficient impact on his consciousness to pro-
voke a specific answer. Perhaps the initial sug-

gestion to give information about any earth changes was still the dominant suggestion, and Hugh Lynn did not sufficiently emphasize that he now wanted only changes that would physically occur in 1934. Whatever the reason, it is clear that Halaliel did not focus on 1934, and he discusses the earth changes as a whole, over many years to come:

Q: *What are the world changes to come this year physically?*
A: The earth will be broken up in many places. The early portion will see a change in the physical aspect of the west coast of America. There will be open waters in the northern portions of Greenland. There will be new lands seen off the Caribbean Sea, and DRY land will appear. There will be the falling away in India of much of the material suffering that has been brought on a troubled people. There will be the reduction of one risen to power in central Europe to naught. The young king son will soon reign [*in Germany*]. In America in the political forces we see a restabilization of the powers of the peoples in their own hands, a breaking up of the rings, the cliques in many places. South America shall be shaken from the uppermost portion to the end, and in the Antarctic off of Tierra Del Fuego LAND, and a strait with rushing waters. (3976-15)

Earlier in this reading you'll notice that the earth changes are to *"begin* in those periods in '58 to '98."* I believe that Halaliel's consciousness was still filled with this information and continued to reveal to us the overall sequence of the changes. Now Hugh Lynn shifts the topic to political issues dealing with Germany and the United States in 1934 and asks a series of questions. He ends with an open question for any more advice:

Q: *Is there any further counsel or advice for us gathered here, which will enable us to understand better our responsibility?*

A: All gathered here in the name of God who is the Father, to those that seek to know His ways—and who is as something outside the veil of their understanding *unless sought!* The counsel of the Father, of that God-Mother comes in each soul that seeks to know the biddings; not as one that would reap vengeance but rather as the loving, MERCIFUL Father. For, as ye show mercy, so may the Father show mercy to thee. As ye show the wisdom, as ye show the love of thy fellow man, so may the love be shown, so may the wisdom, so may the guiding steps day-by-day be shown thee. Be ye joyous in the Lord, knowing that He is ever present with those that seek His face. He is not in heaven, but makes heaven in thine own heart, if ye accept Him. He, God, the Father, is present and manifest in that ye mete to your fellow man in thine own experience.

Would ye know the Father, be the father to thy brother. Would ye know the love of the Father, SHOW thy love to thy faltering, to thy erring brother—but to those that seek, not those that condemn.

We are through. (3976-15)

I cannot throw this material out merely because Halaliel did not correctly address the 1934 physical earth changes question! There is simply too much in this reading that is obviously from a very high source of attunement and guidance. I do not see Halaliel exalting himself or attempting to attract attention to himself. He seems to be directing everyone's attention to God—God within themselves, exactly what Jesus encouraged. The false prophets Jesus warned us about were those that would say the Messiah is over here or there, rather than within us. Halaliel is saying exactly what Jesus taught, that "the kingdom of heaven is within you." These earth-change prophecies should not be ignored because Cayce missed the focusing question about "this year."

Halaliel continues to make appearances in the readings over the next several months of 1934.

On 9 September, the Study Group met again for its seventy-first reading, receiving what they believed to be further information about Halaliel, though it is not clearly stated as such in the reading. Here's what they heard and assumed to be referring to Halaliel:

TO ALL WE WOULD GIVE: Be patient. That part thou hast chosen in such a work is born of truth. Let it come in and be a part of thy daily life. Look in upon the experiences, for, as will be seen, my children, *there has been appointed one that may aid thee in thy future lessons, and he will be thy teacher, thy guide, one sent through the power of thine own desires.* Thine own selves, then, may present his being, meeting, living, dwelling, with thee. *Not the Christ, but His messenger, with the Christ from the beginning, and is to other worlds what the Christ is to this earth.* [my italics] (262-71)

Some in the Study Group, including Hugh Lynn Cayce, wanted to reject Halaliel's help, fearful that they might be led away from Christ. They ultimately did reject his help and asked that only the Christ guide them. Gladys notes that "two or three in the group were still not convinced that we were right in rejecting Halaliel's help in preparing the lessons." Whatever the truth about Halaliel, we hear nothing from him again, and his earth-changes comments are often questioned by those who feel he was not a high source, despite the reading's comments to the contrary. Fortunately, we have many other Cayce readings on earth changes that support and enhance Halaliel's prophecies, as we shall see.

THE GREAT POLE SHIFT

The Halaliel reading that dealt so clearly and specifically with coming earth changes contained a reference to a shifting of the earth's poles. Halaliel said that the changes would begin during the period between 1958 and 1998, but he did not say exactly when the pole shift would occur. During a reading in 1936, Edgar Cayce gives a more exact date. When asked, "What great change or the beginning of what change, if any, is to take place in the Earth in the year A.D. 2000 to 2001?" Cayce answered: "When there is the shifting of the poles; or a new cycle begins." (826-8) The implication in both readings, the Halaliel reading in 1934 and the subsequent reading in 1936, is that a pole shift is an event that develops over a period of some years, beginning in the 1958–1998 range and culminating in the actual shifting in 2000 to 2001, or very near these dates. Controversy surrounds the idea of a pole shift since no one knows what exactly Cayce or Halaliel meant. However, the notion of pole shifts is not new to the earth. How often and how this occurs is unclear. Let's examine what it could be.

The north and south poles of the axis around which our planet spins wobble. Astronomers believe the wobble has been occurring for ages and causes the point of the equinox, as viewed against the backdrop of fixed stars, to move over time. For example, the spring equinox is not viewed against the point of the constellation Aries anymore, it is against the backdrop of the constellation of Pisces. The backward movement of the equinoxes takes approximately 2,166 years per sign, or between twenty-four thousand and twenty-six thousand years to move through the whole cycle of the zodiac. Interestingly, in Hinduism a full day and night of Brahma equals twenty-four thousand years, a Kali-kalpa. In other words, one day in the life of the universe is that long in terms of our years.

There is also the notion of a magnetic shift in the poles. This means that magnetic north can change in a radical fashion. Our geologists have evidence that past magnetic pole shifts have occurred about every one hundred thousand years or so. A magnetic pole shift would cause some tremendous problems with communications and weather, but not necessarily a lot of physical destruction.

However, we could assume that the Van Allen belts that surround our planet would temporarily break down or disappear during the magnetic shift until a realignment of the new magnetic pattern was established. This could be very harmful to life on the planet. The Van Allen belts are magnetic fields that surround the earth and channel incoming radiation from space toward our poles, keeping it from coming into our main living areas on the planet. The luminous bands of the aurora borealis (northern lights) and the aurora australis (southern lights) are the visual signs of these magnetic waves coming down through our atmosphere near our northern and southern poles. It is believed that as a magnetic shift begins, the belts would break up for a time—perhaps a few hours, a few days, a few months or a few years—until the new magnetic poles were established. Then presumably the belts would reestablish their magnetic field around the planet, channeling the incoming radiation to the new poles. During this period the earth would be exposed to increased levels of radiation. Perhaps this is the "fire" that so many prophecies speak of.

In addition, a pole shift could mean that the north pole moves in some way so that it points to an entirely different polestar. (The polestar shows true north since it directly points to our north pole.) On 1 July 1932, Edgar Cayce gave a reading that spoke of a change in the polestar of the earth. He explained that the Great Pyramid of Giza represented the various ages we have been going through. He said, "At the correct time, accurate imaginary lines can be drawn from the opening of the Great Pyramid to the second star in the Great Dipper, called Polaris or the North Star." He must be using the word *Great* as an adjective of importance because Polaris is in the Little Dipper, though it is the second star (SAO 209 is the first).

He continued, "This indicates it is the system toward which the soul takes its flight after having completed its sojourn through this solar system. In October [1932] there will be seen the first variation in the position of the polarstar in relation to the lines from the Great Pyramid. The dipper is gradually changing, and when this change becomes noticeable—as might be calculated from the Pyramid—there will be the beginning of the change in the races [*he's speaking of* root *races, not color races*]. There will come a greater influx of souls from the Atlantean, Lemurian, La, Ur or Da civilizations." (5748-6)

Then he explains that this pyramid was built in this manner by Ra, Hermes and many others who "sought to bring to man a better understanding of the close relationship between the Creative Forces and that created, between man and man, and man and his Maker." Then he cautions that "only those who have been called may truly understand. Who then has been called? Whosoever will make him or herself a channel may be raised to that of a blessing. . . ."

Let's examine the relationship of the entrance to the Great Pyramid and the polestars. There are three polestars for our little blue planet: Thuban, Polaris and Vega. During the time of ancient Egypt, Thuban was the North Star—that is, at midnight above the North Pole, Thuban would have been the northernmost star. Of course, today the North Star is Polaris, and Vega will be the North Star in the future. By extrapolating, I project that Vega will come into position in the year A.D. 10,000. Interestingly, if one draws imaginary lines from the entrance of the Great Pyramid at the spring equinox (about 22–25 March) in 4,000 B.C., A.D. 2,000 and A.D. 10,000, they point directly to the northern star of each age: Thuban, Polaris and Vega, respectively. Hermes, Ra and all the others involved sure knew what they were doing when they built that magnificent monument. But Cayce's discussions of pole shifts obviously refer to a time much closer to the present. The only way for that to happen is a faster pole shift.

Since Polaris indicates "the system toward which the soul takes flight," could the pole change to Vega indicate a new flight pattern? Vega is a blue-white star and the fifth-brightest star in the sky. It is in the constellation Lyra, the harp or lyre of the musician Orpheus. It was said that when Orpheus played this instrument, neither mortal nor god could turn away (Orpheus also introduced reincarnation into Greek mythology, as Cayce did to today's world). Vega also marks the approximate direction toward which our sun and all its planets are traveling through space.

Here's the hard news: In order to have shifted the polestar from Thuban to Polaris, the earth had to shift its northern pole about 26 degrees, not a drastic shift. However, in order to shift the polestar from Polaris to Vega, the earth will have to shift its northern pole a whopping 51 degrees! But if the shift is done gradually over a very long period of time—as Cayce seemed to indicate it would—then we should not expect a dramatic pole shift in 2000 or 2001, just continued pole movement.

On more thing needs to be discussed. References to pole shifts in the Cayce readings may not simply refer to magnetic pole shifts or polestar changes but to a true physical changing of the poles. In other words, the physical planet becomes unstable on its present axis and eventually rolls over and establishes a new axis—the poles literally flip. In this case, there would very likely be destruction to the tectonic plates of the earth, a shifting of the seas, and changes in weather patterns. According to leading scientific teams at major research centers, axis shifts have occurred only every few million or billion years and have taken millions of years to complete.

Whatever the science, for Cayce, the pole shift means the present age is ending and a new one is beginning. Cayce said that during this new age we will regain the powers we had prior to becoming so encased in matter and will be able to use these powers to solve our material needs more easily. Of course, he warns that we had these powers during the time of Atlantis (beginning approximately 212,000 years ago and ending approximately 12,000 years ago) and we did not handle the powers well. Let's hope we've learned something over the past 12,000 years.

EDGAR CAYCE'S GREAT PYRAMID CONNECTION

As we have seen in several readings, Cayce references many events to a timeline recorded in the Great Pyramid at Giza, Egypt. The excavations and research at Giza in the nineteenth and twentieth centuries produced one of the most significant numbers of our time: the pyramid inch. 365.242 of these pyramid inches make up the geometric circle upon which the design of the Great Pyramid is based. It also is the exact number of days in our solar year. As this number continued to appear in different areas of the structure, two English researchers, H. Aldersmith and David Davidson, realized that this special measurement revealed that the Great Pyramid is a stone chronogram, recording a prophetic timeline about coming events. Since one pyramid inch is equal to one year in earth time, Davidson and Aldersmith were able to measure the history of humanity through the pyramid.

On the following pages are diagrams by David Davidson that show how the floor plan of the Great Pyramid prophesies historic time, with time measurement related to the inches within the Great Pyramid. This timeline dates from the Fall from Grace to the year A.D. 2038. Cayce specifically states that these prophecies are not about political movements, but spiritual shifts in humanity's soul growth. Edgar Cayce reading 5748-6 says: "In those conditions that are signified in the way through the pyramid [are the] periods through which the world has passed and is passing, as related to the religious or the spiritual experiences of man."

A number of the Cayce readings reference the pyramid. They came about in the context of the ancient Atlantean and Egyptian period being karmically driven into play again during our lives, with the purposes, powers and souls that were involved then returning to life for another try. Without going into the entire Atlantis/Egypt story, I have tried to include enough of the readings to give you their true perspective. Here Cayce discusses the creation of the pyramid:

Then began the laying out of the pyramid and the building of same. This had begun in those very mountains where they had taken refuge. It was not only built to remain as a place for receiving offers, just as those in the Temple Beauty where upon various altars an individual's innate self was offered, but to be the place of initiation of the initiates.

The pyramid was formed according to the position of various stars around which this particular solar system circles—*going towards what?* Toward

2038

2020

2000
1998

Passage

GRAND GALLERY

S→N

KING'S
CHAMBER

ANTE-CHAMBER

THE COFFER

VERTICAL SECTION (*LOOKING WEST*) OF KING'S CHAMBER: ANTE-CHAMBER AND HOWARD VYSE'S 'CHAMBERS OF CONSTRUCTION' SHOWING 'QUARRY MARKS'. SINGLE SHADE LINES INDICATE LIMESTONE. CROSSED LINES INDICATE GRANITE.

1958

1938

THE KING'S CHAMBER
and
Construction Chambers
(Looking West)

(The Coffer is not in its original position.)

"CHAMBER OF THE OPEN TOMB"
"CHAMBER OF THE TRIPLE VEIL"
ANTECHAMBER (INCLUDING GRANITE LEAF AND BOSS)

NEW AND LIVING WAY
"HALL OF TRUTH IN LIGHT"

KING'S CHAMBER

"CROSSING OF PURE WATERS OF LIFE"—PASSION OF MESSIAH DATE OF CRUCIFIXION A.D. 30 1/4

GRAND GALLERY

2nd LOW PASSAGE
29 May 1928–16 Sept. 1936

GREATSTEP

1st LOW PASSAGE
4 Aug. 1914–11 Nov. 1918

QUEEN'S CHAMBER

HORIZONTAL PASSAGE

FIRST ASCENDING

ACCESS TO
"CHAMBER OF SECOND BIRTH" OR "NEW BIRTH"

18 Jan. 1918

4 B.C.
BIRTH OF CHRIST

"CHAMBER OF CHAOS"
"UPSIDE-DOWNNESS"

SUBTERRANEAN CHAMBER

LATER TUNNELED INSPECTION SHAFT

DESCENDING PASSAGE

Descending Passage: The Scientific Data symbolize "Upside-downness" during Spiritual descent.

20 July 1926

Words thus:—GRAND GALLERY refer to the Modern Names for passages and chambers.
Words thus:—NEW AND LIVING WAY refer to Davidson's correlation to the Bible.
Words thus:—"HALL OF TRUTH IN LIGHT" "CROSSING OF PURE WATERS OF LIFE" refer to the designations in the Egyptian Book of the Dead.

The Pyramid face produced to meet 1st Ascending Passage produced defines the point corresponding to Autumnal Equinox 4000 B.C.

The Sacred Line date defines that the Pyramid's year begins at the Autumnal Equinox and its day at Midnight.

The Sacred Line points to Alcyoné of Pleides and the Entrance Passage Axis to Pole Star 2144 B.C.

The Scored Line does not give the date of the Pyramid's construction. The Pyramid was built between 3000 and 2500 B.C.

The Pyramid was designed and originally set out with its arris edges and hollowed-in face as shown; the difference between the two base square circuits being the value of the Pyramid's Mathematical "Displacement Factor."

HOLLOWED-IN FACE

PLANE OF ARRIS EDGES

DATE OF PASSAGE PERPENDICULAR AT PLANE OF ARRIS EDGES 2644 B.C.

TO POLE STAR 2144 B.C.

"HALL OF TRUTH IN DARKNESS" ISRAEL UNDER "YOKE OF THE LAW"

ENTRANCE TO PYRAMID

PASSAGE

GRANITE PLUG

SCORED LINE 2144 B.C.

"GATE OF ASSENT"

1000 B.C.   EXODUS DATE 1486 B.C.

Ascending Passage produced:
The Scientific Data symbolize the promise of ascent even while descent (symbolized by the Entrance Passage) was taking place, i.e., between 2644 B.C. and 1486 B.C.

4000 B.C. HISTORY OF ADAMIC RACE BEGINS

The Egyptian Government Survey (1925) gives the hollowed-in base square circuit precisely as (36,524-2465-286-1022) Pyramid inches: 36,524-2465 being the mean historical value of the solar year in days x 100; and 286-1022 being the Pyramid's Mathematical "Displacement Factor." The latter value is the Key to the Demonstration of the Great Pyramid's Science and its Prophetic Purpose.

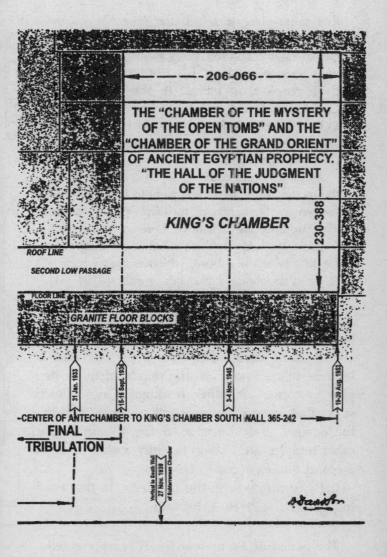

that same place to which the priest [*in ancient Egypt, Edgar Cayce had been the priest Ra-Ta*] was banished—the constellation of Libra, or to Libya were these people sent. Is it not fitting then, that these people must return? As this priest [*Edgar Cayce*] may develop himself to be in that position to be a LIBERATOR of the world in its relationships to individuals in those periods to come; for he must enter again in that period, or in 1998.

As the changes come about in the earth, those things that were preserved were to later be made known in the minds of those peoples to come. The rise and fall of nations were to be depicted in this same temple which acted as an interpreter for that which had been, which is, and which is to be in the material plane. [my italics] (294-151)

There are many strange and curious statements in this reading. I particularly noted the comment about "those things that were preserved were to later be made known in the minds of those peoples to come." In other readings, Cayce clearly states that we are "those people to come" and that the images and concepts in the pyramids and other temples are to help us fully realize who we are and what we are to be doing.

Let's continue with the readings. In this reading given 1 July 1932, he said:

The period of the present [*1932*] is represented by the low passage or depression showing a downward tendency, as indicated by the variations in the character of stone used. This might be termed in the present as the Cruciatarian Age [cruciat *means a crusade, and often was used with the word* torturing *or* tormenting, *such as* cruciatory torturing], or that in which preparations are being made *for the beginning of a new sub-race,* or a change, which—as indicated from the astronomical or numerical conditions—dates from the latter portion or middle portion of the present fall [1932]. In October, there will be a period in which the benevolent influences of Jupiter and Uranus will be stronger, which—from an astrological viewpoint—will bring a greater interest in occult or mystic influences. At the correct time, accurate imaginary lines can be drawn from the opening of the Great Pyramid to the second star in the Great Dipper, called Polaris or the North Star. This indicates it is the system toward which the soul takes its flight after having completed its sojourn through this solar system. In October, there will be seen the first variation in the position of the polarstar in relation to the lines from the Great Pyramid. The dipper is gradually changing, and when this change becomes noticeable—as might be calculated from the Pyramid—there will be *the beginning of the change in the races.* There will come a greater influx of souls from the Atlantean, Lemurian, La, Ur or Da civilizations.

These conditions are indicated in this turn in the journey through the Pyramid.

How was this begun? Who was given that this should be a record of man's experiences in this root race? For that is the period covered by the prophecies in the pyramid. This was given by Ra and Hermes in that period during the reign of Araaraart when there were many who sought to bring to man a better understanding of the close relationship between the Creative Forces and that created, between man and man, and man and his Maker.

Only those who have been called may truly understand. Who then has been called? Whosoever will make himself a channel may be raised to that of a blessing. That is all that entity-body is able to comprehend. Who, having his whole measure full, would desire more does so to his own undoing.

Q: *What definite details are indicated as to what will happen after we enter the period of the King's Chamber?*

A: When the bridegroom is at hand, all do rejoice. When we enter that understanding of being in the King's presence, with that of the mental seeking—the joy, the buoyancy, the new understanding, the new life, through the period.

Q: *What is the significance of the empty sarcophagus?*

A: That there will be no more death. Don't misunderstand or misinterpret! But the INTERPRETATION of death will be made plain.

Q: *If the Armageddon is foretold in the Great Pyramid, please give a description of it and the date of its beginning and ending.*

A: Not in what is left there. It will be as a thousand years, with the fighting in the air, and between those returning to and those leaving the earth.

Q: *What is the date, as recorded by the Pyramid, of entering in the King's Chamber?*

A: '38 to '58 [*notice how Davidson has it as '36 to '53*]. [my italics] (5748-6)

Cayce goes on to say that when we reach the far wall of the King's Chamber, we are to proceed up the wall, something Davidson never realized. Cayce instructs us in 5748-5 to also notice the variations in stone, color, layers, markings and turns as we make "passage through same, from the base to the top—to the open tomb AND the top." All of these variations indicate changes in "religious thought in the world." Notice how this is measured in the third illustration. From the floor of the King's Chamber to the top is from 1958 to approximately 2038.

When Cayce was asked in this reading, "Are the deductions and conclusions arrived at by D. Davidson and H. Aldersmith in their book on the

Great Pyramid correct?" he answered, "Many of these that have been taken as deductions are correct. Many are far overdrawn. Only an initiate may understand." Finally, when asked, "In which pyramid are the records of the Christ?" he answered, "That is yet to be uncovered."

Key to Cayce's vision of these times is his continual reference to a new sub-race or human body type. Cayce stated that this body we use today is the fourth body type used by incarnating souls. He states that a new body type is in the makings, a fifth one, that will allow our souls more illumination and greater sensory perception. He states that the pyramid chronogram runs only until this new body is formed. Apparent in his readings are identifiable stages leading to this event.

Cayce further states:

The apex of the pyramid (which has long since been removed by the sons of Heth [*the sons of Noah's son Ham in Genesis 10:15*]), was of metal. It was to be indestructible, being of copper, brass and gold with other alloys.

Gizeh was to be the place of the initiates and their gaining understanding by personal application and the journeys through various activities in the earth. Then it was fitting that the placing of the crown on the pyramid, this symbol of the record, was done by one who represented both the old and the new; one representing the Sons of the Law in Atlantis, Lemuria, Oz and Og. So, Hept-supht, he who keeps the record shut, was chosen as the one to seal that in the tomb.

The old record in Gizeh is from the journey to the Pyrenees to the death of the Son of Man, as a man, and then to 1998. (378-14)

In this reading we are told of "a journey to the Pyrenees, to the death of the Son of Man, as a man, and then to 1998." As we continue in this book, we will see how the Pyrenees are also a part of the Nostradamus and Divine Feminine material. Apparently, humanity took a major turn in its development as it reached that area. The death of the Son of Man as a man, is clearly seen by Cayce as another key transition toward this new body. In or near 1998, we will take another step toward this body. Since the last timeline date in the Great Pyramid is A.D. 2038, we can assume that this new sub-race will be completed in or near that date, though Cayce says that the body types will overlap, some still having a fourth body type while others have the new one.

1998: CAYCE'S YEAR OF GREAT EVENTS AND BEYOND

As the Cayce pyramid and other readings show, Cayce makes numerous references to the year 1998. In the pyramid readings, 1998 seems to mark the beginning of a shift. Other Cayce readings also specifically refer to 1998. For example, a seeker who is familiar with Jacob Boehme's work asks the "sleeping" Cayce a series of questions about the Aquarian Age and also gets the 1998 date:

Q: *Is the gradual restoration of phosphorus in man so he will talk back and forth with Cosmos, like the radio principle?*

A: This is gradually a development of which the awareness of the use of the spiritual consciousness may be a medium through which such may be done.

Q: *What does the restoration of phosphorus signify?*

A: The relationship of the individual to that awareness of the Universal Consciousness, which is the promise of all who have wholly put on Him. For as He has given, "he that abideth wholly in me and I in him, to him will be made aware all things from the foundations of the world." This is ALL there, in His words, in His promises to man [*John 14–17*]. Just as indicated in His exhortation upon the revelation activities of John, and as to what they meant in the affairs of man. That place, that awareness. And yet, when individuals will, even as John, become aware of being within the presence of Life itself, God Himself made manifest, how few accepted it?

Q: *What will the Aquarian Age mean to mankind as regards Physical, Mental and Spiritual development?*

A: These are as growths. In the center of the Piscean Age we had the entrance of "Emmanuel" or God among men, see? What did that mean? The same will be meant by the full consciousness of the ability to communicate with the Creative Forces, and the uses of same in material environs.

This awareness in the age of Atlantis and Lemuria brought what? The destruction of man, and his beginning of the journey up through selfishness.

Q: *Why is the Aquarian Age described as the "Age of the Lily?"*

A: The purity. Only the purity as it represents will be able to comprehend or understand that awareness that is before those who seek the way.

Q: *Can a date be given to indicate the beginning of the Aquarian Age?*

A: It laps over from one to another, as he holds to that which has been, which is—as has been indicated, we will begin to understand fully in '98.

Q: *Three hundred years ago Jacob Boehme decreed Atlantis would rise again at this crisis time when we cross from this Piscean Era into the Aquarian. Is Atlantis rising now? Will it cause a sudden convolution and about what year?*

A: In 1998 we may find a great deal of the activities as have been wrought by the gradual changes that are coming about. These are at the periods when the cycle of the solar activity, or the years as related to the sun's passage through the various spheres of activity become paramount to the change between the Piscean and the Aquarian Age. This is a *gradual*, not a cataclysmic activity in the experience of the earth in this period. (1602-3)

Ms. 1602 is an amazing seeker, and her questioning of the "sleeping" Cayce has brought us some important information. As we have seen, the End Times prophecies include many comments about our bodies being changed. Here Ms. 1602 gets Cayce to identify that phosphorus is rising in our bodies and will someday be sufficient for us to "become aware of being within the presence of Life itself, God Himself made manifest." She also gets Cayce to identify one of the primary qualities of this new era. Saying the last era was "God among men," Cayce says this coming era will be "the full consciousness of the ability to communicate with the Creative

Forces, and the uses of same in material environs."

Continuing with the 1998 readings, we have a father hoping that he and his family can join with Cayce on his return during this great era:

Q: *Will I, or any of my immediate family, reincarnate with Mr. Cayce in 1998?*
A: This is not to be given, or things of such a nature, but is to be determined by the desire, the need, the application of those who may desire to do so. (2285-1)

Finally, we have a reading that is truly remarkable for its clear dating of the return of the Messiah. I found it curious that Cayce chose that term to identify this coming Being. It seems to indicate a universalness to the coming, rather than the specific religion-connected term "Christ." Of course, even Christ said he had flocks beyond the one he came to. Here's the reading, again referencing the Great Pyramid and the Xerxes material we discussed in the previous chapter:

In this same pyramid did the Great Initiate, the Master, take those last of the Brotherhood degrees with John, the forerunner of Him, at that place. As is indicated in that period where entrance is shown to be in that land that was set apart, as that promised to that peculiar peoples, as were rejected—as is shown in that portion when there is the turning back from the raising up of Xerxes as the deliverer from an unknown tongue or land, and again is there seen that this occurs in the entrance of the Messiah in this period—1998. (5748-5)

Obviously the year 1998 is a significant one from Edgar Cayce's perspective. Nostradamus viewed 1999 as a key marker. Frankly, these two seers were so close in their timing for a significant change close to the end of the millennium that a one-year variation does not amount to much in my opinion.

There is also the Mayans' prophecy that our current age, which they called "the age of movement," ends in December 2012, and Cayce's Great Pyramid timeline, which ends in 2038 (more on this later). Clearly the years from 1998 through to 2038 are when much of this prophesied change is to occur.

EDGAR CAYCE'S EARTH-CHANGE PREDICTIONS

An additional point of significance about the year 1998 is that it seems to have been central to many of Cayce's more famous earth-change predictions. These predictions have to do with significant disruption in the geopolitical map of the world as we know it. Though these predictions may not have come to pass, it remains to be seen whether they will yet be fulfilled. One thing is clear: major disruptions of some kind marks the beginning of the End Times in the Cayce readings.

There are so many Cayce predictions of dramatic change, so I've listed only the major ones here. This first reading occurs on 20 January 1936, two years after the Halaliel readings ended. As you can see, Cayce is still conveying a vision of major changes for our world. This is a personal reading for Mr. 270, dealing with many personal issues, but toward the end of the reading, 270 asks the following question:

Q: *What is the primary cause of earthquakes? Will San Francisco suffer from such a catastrophe this year [1936]? If so, give date, time and information for the guidance of this body, who has personal property, records and a wife, all of which it wishes safety.*

A: We do not find that this particular district [*San Francisco*] in the present year [*1936*] will suffer the great MATERIAL damages that HAVE been experienced heretofore. While portions of the country will be affected, we find

these will be farther EAST than San Francisco—
or those SOUTH, where there has NOT been
heretofore the greater activity.

The causes of earthquakes, of course, are the
movements of the earth; that is, internally. And,
the cosmic activity or influence of other plane-
tary forces and stars produce the activities of
the elementals of the earth; that is, the Earth,
the Air, the Fire, the Water—and those combi-
nations make for the replacements in the various activities.

If there are the greater activities in the Vesuvius, or Pelée, then the southern coast of California—and the areas between Salt Lake and the
southern portions of Nevada—may expect,
within the three months following the greater
activity, an inundation by the earthquakes. But
these, as we find, are to be more in the southern
than in the northern hemisphere. (270-35)

This fits very well with Halaliel's prophecy,
"The earth will be broken up in the western portion of America." Obviously the Cayce readings
are predicting significant changes for America;
most of the drastic changes will be in South
America, but North America will have its share.
The changes to the western coast of North
America are apparently triggered by the two
volcanoes, Vesuvius in Italy and Pelée on the
island of Martinique in the West Indies.

In 1941, Cayce gave another detailed description of the prophesied earth changes:

As to conditions in the geography of the world, of the country, changes are gradually coming about.

In the next few years lands will appear in the Atlantic as well as in the Pacific. And what is the coastline of many a land now will be the bed of the ocean. Even many of the battlefields of the present [*World War II in 1941*] will be ocean, will be the seas, the bays, the lands over which the *new* order will carry on their trade.

Portions of the now east coast of New York, or New York City itself, will disappear. This will be another generation though. The southern portions of Carolina, Georgia will disappear. [*Could he be referring to movement along the major fault in Charleston, South Carolina?*] This will come first.

The waters of the lakes [*Great Lakes*] will empty into the Gulf [*of Mexico*] rather than the waterway over which such discussions have been recently made [*St. Lawrence Seaway*]. It would be well if the new waterway were prepared.

Then the area where the entity is now located [*Virginia Beach*] will be among the safety lands, as will be what is now Ohio, Indiana and Illinois and much of the southern portion of Canada and the eastern portion of Canada. While, the western land is to be disturbed. (1152-11)

Ms. 1152 finishes this reading with some very direct questions about New York City, Los Angeles and San Francisco.

Q: *I have for many months felt that I should move away from New York City.*
A: This is well. There is too much unrest. There will continue to be the character of vibrations that to this body will be disturbing. Eventually, there will be the destructive forces there—though these will be in the next generation.
Q: *Will Los Angeles be safe?*
A: Los Angeles, San Francisco, most all of these will be among those that will be destroyed before New York even. (1152-11)

While Cayce predicts destruction in New York, in the next generation, did this mean he predicted the 11 September 2001 attack on the World Trade Center? But he also predicted that Los Angeles and San Francisco would be among those cities destroyed *before* New York. Clearly this has not come to pass.

In 1942, a person asked if their business location would be safe until their lease expired. The answer was that those locations on the mainland would be safe, but not those on Manhattan Island (412-13). The trouble with this reading is that the lease in question was for only one year, expiring in 1943, and Manhattan Island was still there at the lease expiration. Is this another example of a vision of the future affecting Cayce's deeper consciousness so profoundly that it cannot relate to the one-year time frame of the question? Or is it simply a mistake?

I outline below the main earth changes as described by Cayce:

- Much of the West Coast, the Carolina and Georgia southern coast, and the New England coast of the United States will be changed by earthquakes.
- Within ninety days of greater activity in either of the two volcanoes Pelée or Vesuvius, powerful earthquakes will cause an inundation from the Great Salt Lake through southern portions of Nevada to the southern coast of California.
- Land will rise off the Atlantic and Pacific coasts of the United States.
- Los Angeles, San Francisco and eventually New York will be destroyed by earthquakes.
- New York will be rebuilt around the year 2158 a little west of where it is today.

- The Great Lakes will empty into the Gulf of Mexico.
- The United States will experience food shortages.
- Ultimately Livingston, Montana, will be one of the breadbaskets of the world, as will be the pampas of Argentina and parts of Africa!
- Most of the serious earthquake changes will occur in the southern hemisphere.
- Europe will be physically changed quickly.
- A new people will conduct trade on seas that will cover the battlefields of World War II.
- The poles will shift between the years 2000 and 2001.
- Climates will change, especially cold areas becoming warmer.
- The greater portion of Japan will go into the sea.
- China will become the bedrock of Christianity (though it will be a very long time before this happens).
- Out of Russia will come the hope of the world. In stating this, Cayce implies that it will be done by some cooperative relationship with the United States.
- Volcanic eruptions will increase in the torrid area around the equator.

- There will be a return to the land for mankind.
- After the earth changes, people will not build huge megalopolises like we presently have from Washington, D.C., to Boston. Rather, industries will be spread out across the countryside.
- Safety lands will be Ohio, Illinois, Indiana, Virginia and portions of southern Canada. Of course, he indicates Montana and some portions of the Great Plains, such as Nebraska, will be safe.
- The power center of the world will always be in Washington, D.C.

Of some comfort in the face of these predictions is the following reading referencing a dream that Cayce had about the earth changes:

Q: *Interpret and explain the dream Edgar Cayce had on March 3, 1936, in which he was born again over two hundred years in the future and traveled to various sections of the country where records of Edgar Cayce could be found.*

A: This then is the interpretation. As has been given, "Fear not." Keep the faith; for those that be with thee are greater than those that would hinder. Though the very heavens fall, though the earth shall be changed, though the heavens shall pass, the promises in Him are sure and will stand—as in that day—as the proof of thy activity in the lives and hearts of those of thy fellow man.

For indeed and in truth ye know, "As ye do it unto thy fellow man, ye do it unto thy God, to thyself." For, SELF effaced, God may indeed glorify thee and make thee STAND as one that is called for a purpose in the dealings, the relationships, with thy fellow man. Be not unmindful that he is nigh unto thee in every trial, in every temptation, and hath not willed that thou should perish.

Make thy will then one with His. Be not afraid.

That is the interpretation. That the periods from the material angle as visioned are to come to pass matters not to the soul, but do thy duty TODAY! TOMORROW will care for itself.

These changes in the earth will come to pass, for the time and times and a half are at an end, and there begin those periods for the readjustments. For how hath He given? "The righteous shall inherit the earth."

Hast thou, my brethren, a heritage in the earth? (294-185)

The reading says that these changes "begin those periods [of] readjustments," indicating the readjustments will fulfill the prophecy that "the

righteous shall inherit the earth." (Matt. 5:10)
However, the reading also gives clear instructions to those of us living prior to the changes or in the midst of them: "Fear not" and "keep the faith." We are admonished to remember that, "The periods from the material angle as visioned are to come to pass matters not to the soul, but do thy duty TODAY! TOMORROW will care for itself." In other words, worry about today rather than about what is to come. Finally, we are told, "Make thy will one with His. Be not afraid."

ARMAGEDDON

As we have seen, the Cayce readings contain many references to the biblical prophecies about the End Times. Perhaps the most amazing one is his bold statement in the previous section that "the time, times and half a time" spoken of in the prophet Daniel's vision are over! Clearly this means that the End Times are upon us. There can be no other interpretation of such a statement. In fact, the Edgar Cayce readings repeatedly state that the time, times and half a time are over.

The end of the time, times and half a time means that a great battle is about to take place between the forces of the light and good and the forces of the darkness and evil. So, for Cayce, the end of the time, times and half a time is the beginning of the last great battle of Armageddon, which will be followed by the thousand years of peace with "Satan bound." You may recall how Halaliel referenced this period in his earth-change reading:

And those that in the inmost recesses of their selves awaken to the spiritual truths that are to be given, and those places that have acted in the capacity of teachers among men, the rottenness of those that have ministered in places will be brought to light, and turmoils and strifes shall enter. And, as there is the wavering of those that would enter as emissaries, as teachers, from the throne of life, the throne of light, the throne of immortality, and wage war in the air with those of darkness, *then know ye the Armageddon is at hand.* For with the great numbers of the gathering of the hosts of those that have hindered and would make stumbling blocks for man and his weaknesses, *they shall wage war with the spirits of light that come into the earth for this awakening*; that have been and are being called by those of the sons of men into the service of the living God. For He, as ye have been told, is not the God of the dead, not the God of those that have forsaken Him, but those that love His coming, that love His associations among men—the God of the LIVING, the God of Life! For, He IS Life. [my italics] (3976-15)

There are two more references to the Armageddon in the Cayce readings. One relates to the Great Pyramid in Giza and the other to the spirituality of the American people.

Q: *If the Armageddon is foretold in the Great Pyramid, please give a description of it and the date of its beginning and ending.*
A: Not in what is left there. *It will be as a thousand years, with the fighting in the air, and— as has been—between those returning to and those leaving the earth.* [my italics] (5748-6)

This certainly fits with the previous reading in which Halaliel describes Armageddon as a battle between "those that would enter as emissaries, as teachers, from the throne of life, the throne of light, the throne of immortality, and wage war in the air with those of darkness." It is also important to note that the Armageddon is to last a thousand years. Hopefully the end of this war is near, and the thousand years of peace will begin soon.

Cayce cautions that peace depends on the spirituality of the American people—an idea the relevance of which is even more important than ever. In October 1926, after the end of World War I, the following reading cautioned that without spirituality and brotherhood, there will again come Armageddon. Unfortunately, World War II was not far in coming.

These are rather the conditions as may be expected: The spirituality of the American people will be the criterion of that as is to become the world's forces. As has been given in that of the peace table [*the 1919 Treaty of Versailles, ending World War I*], there sat the Master in the American people [*through President Woodrow Wilson and his group*], with the brotherhood of the world accepted—war was at an end. Without same [*spirituality and the brotherhood of the world*] there will again come the Armageddon [*World War II?*], and in same there will be seen that the Christian forces will AGAIN move westward. [my italics] (900-272)

Here we are in the new millenium, and the United States is a survivor of the hot and cold wars of the 1900s. Is our spirituality intact? Do we still hold to the brotherhood of the world?

A NOAH-LIKE TIME

There is a fascinating reading for a woman who was on Noah's ark, but in the reading Cayce gives some further insights into the coming changes and their relationship to the changes that occurred during Noah's time. You'll recall, even Jesus references Noah on the Mount of Olives. The reading begins with Cayce's mind looking over this woman's Book of Life, her records on the skein of time and space:

What an unusual record—and one of those who might be termed as physically "the mothers of the world!" Because the entity was one of those in Noah's ark.

The entity has appeared when there were new revelations to be given. And again it appears when there are new revelations to be made.

May the entity so conduct its mind, its body and its purposes, then, as to be a channel through which such messages may come that are needed for the awakenings in the minds of men as to the necessity for returning to the search for their relationship with the Creative Forces or God.

For as has been given from the beginning, the deluge [Noah's flood] was not a myth (as many would have you believe) but a period when man had so belittled himself with the cares of the world, with the deceitfulness of his own knowledge and power, as to require that there be a return to his dependence wholly—physically and mentally—upon the Creative Forces.

Will this entity see such again occur in the earth? Will it be among those who may be given directions as to how, where, the elect may be preserved for the replenishing again of the earth?

Remember, not by water—for it is the mother of life in the earth—but rather by the elements, fire. (3653-1)

This is a disturbing reading. It seems to say that there will be a new destruction, like the one that occurred during Noah's period, yet this time it will be by fire, not water. And it also seems to say that the destruction will be of such a magnitude that we'll be "given directions as to how, where, the elect may be preserved for the replenishing again of the earth"!

I know many of us hate these doom prophecies. They are so awesome that it appears impossible to live our daily lives with them hanging over our heads. All I can trust in—with my own wife, children and hopes for this life—is Jesus' teaching that with God *all things are possible*. It's also important to realize that this reading does clearly indicate that life will go on, as it did after Noah.

The fire mentioned in this reading could possibly come from the increase in radiation as the Van Allen belts break down during a shift of the magnetic poles. This would be "like a fire" and would affect the whole earth.

On the whole, the Cayce readings are positive and encouraging about the future and its potential.

REINCARNATION AND SOUL GROUPS

As you know, Edgar Cayce taught that reincarnation was occurring. He gave many readings for people in which he explained that current situations in their lives were due to the activities of their souls in past incarnations, even if the persons did not remember or know about them. He stated that the soul had karma, challenges to meet in this life that were caused by actions in past lives. He also taught that souls travel in what he called soul groups. Since many of his predictions about wars dealt with the karma of these soul groups, let's look at what he said about the tensions between the Middle Eastern and Western soul groups.

One could consider the 2001 terrorist attacks on the United States in the context of these Cayce teachings. Cayce would suggest that these are not just current events, but undoubtedly have past motivations and karma behind them. Amazingly, in specific readings Cayce spoke of the Crusades, which occurred nearly one thousand years ago, and pointed to them as the beginning of the tensions between Middle Eastern and Western peoples, or soul groups. The Crusades were some of the bloodiest battles in history.

Of the many past-life readings Edgar Cayce gave over the years, 102 were for souls who had incarnated, both as Christians and Muslims, during the times of the holy wars between Muslims and Christians. In some of his readings, he referred to the crusaders as "zealous ones" (355-1) who came to take back the Holy City from perceived heathens, but found in their contacts with the Muslims that the Muslims had a brotherly love and showed it to many crusaders who were captured or injured and came under their care. The readings also reveal that the crusaders also learned that these "infidels" had a science and hygiene that was in many respects superior to that of the crusaders.

In all his readings, Cayce never wavered from the principle of oneness and brotherhood of all peoples: "For whether they be Greek, Parthenian, Jew or Gentile—whether they be of Mohammed, Confucius, or even Shinto or On or Mu— the Lord, thy God, is ONE! For all force, all power that is manifested in thyself, is of the

ONE source." (1494-1) In another he said, "Let that rather be thy watchword, 'I am my brother's keeper.' Who is thy brother? Whoever, wherever he is, that bears the imprint of the Maker in the earth, be he black, white, gray or grizzled, be he young, be he Hottentot, or on the throne or in the president's chair. All that are in the earth today are thy brothers. Those that have gradually forgotten God entirely have been eliminated, and there has come—now— and will come at the close of this next year— the period when there will be no part of the globe where man has not had the opportunity to hear, 'The Lord He is God.' And, as has been indicated, *when this period has been accomplished, then the new era, the new age, is to begin.* Will ye have a part of it, or will ye let it pass by and be merely a hanger-on, or one upon whom your brother—the Lord, thy Christ—may depend?" (2780-3). My italics emphasize an important point to remember.

Cayce also cautioned against war out of anger or revenge. He told one former crusader, "Yet in those periods the entity learned much: that they who fight, they who war against their brethren find themselves warring as against the spirit of truth. For that as is sown in anger, that as is sown in dread, must be reaped in turmoil and in strife." (1226-1)

EDGAR CAYCE'S PROPHECIES END POSITIVELY

Because so much of Cayce's material is about earthquakes, volcanoes and wars, he is often considered one of the prophets of doom. But he clearly states that all of these changes are necessary in order to clean up unfinished business or karma, both within individual souls and among soul groups. The new age that follows these changes is a wonderful age of enlightenment, love and cooperation. He repeats the statement in the Revelation that during this future age "Satan will be bound," meaning that all evil will be in check. But the new age cannot be entered until all the negative, evil influences within us are cleansed. This is a concept that we'll see in the prophecies of the Virgin Mary, in which she, too, states that there will be a "chastisement." It is in the biblical prophecies: "Whom God loves, He chastens." (Heb. 12:6) If the Cayce prophecies are correct, the way to this new era of bound evil and illuminating love and light is a challenging one.

3

THE PROPHECIES OF NOSTRADAMUS

In the year 1555, Michel de Nostradame (A.D. 1503–1566) published the first edition of his prophetic book series, *Centuries.* He was already a well-known author, having published an annual almanac since 1550, and was famed for his cure for the Black Death (plague) of the Middle Ages. However famous he was in his lifetime, it did not compare to the fame he has gained since his death.

Now known throughout the world as "Nostradamus," he was born to Jewish parents in a Europe under the dark, suspicious gaze of the Inquisition. His parents raised him Roman Catholic, but converted Jews were highly suspect to the Inquisitors. And although he was a doctor trained at the best medical school of his time, he was not readily accepted by his peers. Those were the days when medicine was dominated by the practice of bloodletting with leeches, which Nostradamus openly refused to do, choosing to treat patients with clean drinking water, clean bathing water, clean garments and bedding, herbs and rose hip pills of his own making, which were as popular then as our vitamin C pills are today. When you combine his questionable religious legitimacy and his questionable medical practices with his prophesying, he was in very grave danger of the fear and suspicion of the people of his time. Nostradamus once wrote, "Here where I reside, I carry on my work among animals, barbarians, mortal enemies of learning and letters." If it were not for his success with curing plague victims and prophesying accurately for the royal families in secular power, he probably would have been burned at the stake of the Inquisition. When you consider that he was certainly practicing an ancient, and mostly pagan, method of divination in order to receive his visions, he was, according to the Inquisition's list of evils, a perfect example of the evil that "must be purged from our presence." Fortunately, they never quite got their hands on him. He died, as he prophesied, on 2 July 1566, in the exact position and manner that he had foreseen.

In the beginning of *Centuries* series he describes his method as follows:

Seated alone in secret study
Alone it rests on the brazen tripod
A slender flame licks out of the solitude
Making possible that which would otherwise
    have been vain.

The wand in his hand is placed between the
    branches
He moistens the hem of his garment and his
    foot
Fear arises and a voice sets him trembling in
    his robes
In divine splendor, a god sits nearby.

Century 1, Quatrains 1 & 2

Anyone familiar with the manuscripts *De Mysteriis Egyptorum* by Iamblichus, *De Demonibus* by Michael Psellus and the legendary *The Key of Solomon*—all forbidden by the Inquisition—would know that these two quatrains reveal a knowledge of the specific methods used in these manuscripts for the evocation of spirits. To be in possession of one of these manuscripts was enough to put you to the torture of the Inquisitors. To be actually using the guidance in

these works would send you to the stake. There
is little doubt that Nostradamus was using his
modified version of ancient methods for conjur-
ing up the forces and conditions necessary for
him to see the visions. The "it" in the second
line of the first quatrain was either a black mirror (a black concave piece of polished metal) or
a tray of specially prepared water into which he
would gaze. He wrote to his son that the visions
came to him in the manner of "imaginative impression" revealed by "God Almighty." Imaginative impression may be exactly what Edgar
Cayce was trying to teach to his followers when
he encouraged them to develop the "imaginative forces."[1]

In this next quatrain, notice how Nostradamus
warns all readers, but notice also that, though
he pays homage to the Christian power of his
time—and there's much evidence that he genu-
inely was a believer in Christ—he also allows
for other practitioners as long as they are "priest
of the rite"—in other words, initiates into the
secret teachings and methods.

Let those who read these quatrains reflect
  maturely
Let the profane, the vulgar and the common
  herd be kept away
Let all—idiot astrologers, non-Christians—stay
  distant

Who does otherwise, let them be priest of the
rite.

6:100

Since he was himself an astrologer, the third
line must refer to ignorant, mundane astrologers
without a clear vision of the cosmos, not all astrologers. We know that Nostradamus prayed,
fasted, donned special garments and went through
an elaborate preparation ceremony before beginning to gaze into the future—all the trappings
of a "priest of the rite."

THE PROBLEM INTERPRETING
HIS PROPHECIES

Nostradamus deliberately obscured his prophecies. His quatrains (four-line poems) are not in
any sequential order, making it very difficult to
establish a clear time line for the events and to
get the whole picture on any particular event or
series of events. One literally has to go through
the nearly one thousand quatrains and find everything that appears to refer to a singular major
event, such as the Second World War, and then,
putting them together, try to establish the sequence of events and people involved. In addition to the jumbled arrangement of the
quatrains, he deliberately modified names and

places using anagrams or ancient and foreign
language names for these people and places. So,
though he wrote mostly in French, his quatrains
are peppered with Latin, Greek and several
other languages. His anagrams for the names of
people and places are difficult to see with foresight, but much easier to see with hindsight. For
example, he sees a new country coming in the
distant future (he's viewing in the mid 1500s,
seeing into the mid 1700s) and calls this country
l'Americh, unmistakably America; he calls a future leader *Hister* and *Ister*, which most believe
is a reference to Hitler; and the strange name
Pau Nay Loron is likely the anagram for *Napaulon
Roy* or *Napoleon the King*.

In the preface to *Centuries*, Nostradamus says
that he wrote his quatrains "in dark and ab-
struse sayings . . . under a cloudy figure" for
fear of controversy. And I would add: the dan-
gers of a people so afraid of the unknown that
they tended to kill it rather than try to understand it. In fact, Nostradamus was once nearly
killed by a mob spooked by his accurate foresight into the death of their king, Henry II. This
was the quatrain:

The young lion will overcome the old one
In single combat on a field of battle
In a golden cage his eyes will be pierced

Two wounds as one, followed by a cruel death.

1:35[2]

The old lion was known in his lifetime to be King Henry II, who used the emblem of the lion (line 1). Shortly after the publication of this quatrain, King Henry II was killed during a joust (line 2) in which his opponent was a young Scottish captain who also used the emblem of the lion. The young captain's lance splintered upon impact and a piece went through the visor of the golden helmet (*cage*, line 3) of the old king, piercing his eye and brain, causing him to die a slow and painful death over the next ten days (line 4). An angry mob ran through the streets of Paris, looking to burn the prophet for his accuracy—the old kill-the-messenger approach to bad news. Fortunately, Henry's queen was a strong supporter of Nostradamus, so he was spared. The queen turned all attention upon the captain's role in the death of the king, and it was the captain who had to escape to England for fear of his life.

Still it was considered by everyone to be a most accurate prophecy, causing Nostradamus to gain the mixed blessing of fame and suspicion of sorcery. He was right to try to obscure his prophecies so that only those who had the training and wisdom could decipher them.

I am not going to make something out of quatrains that are simply too difficult to interpret. Fortunately, there are many quatrains that are very clear in their meaning and to whom and what they refer. It is these quatrains on which we will focus our attention.

I have divided the selected prophecies into four sections: 1) Those dealing with the Antichrist, because this figure is always associated with the End Times, 2) Those dealing with heavenly signs, because even Jesus references the signs in the heavens as signposts of coming changes, 3) Those dealing with the sequence of popes and their relevance to the End Times and finally 4) earth changes.

THE PROPHECIES OF ANTICHRIST

Most interpreters of Nostradamus's quatrains agree that he foresaw three great Antichrists, namely: Napoleon, Hitler and someone named *Mabus* and/or *Alus*, which are most certainly anagrams or coded versions of the real name or names. Without a doubt, Napoleon and Hitler were destroyers of the world Nostradamus knew—all of Europe, England, Russia, Scandinavia and North Africa felt the sting of their war machines. Each leader fit the prophecies that stated that the Antichrist would always appear to be a godsend in the beginning of his reign, and the masses would rally behind him with great hope and expectations, only to see him turn into a demanding tyrant who would tolerate no opposition and send their children into bloody battles of unclear purpose until the death counts were so shocking as to numb the surviving population. Napoleon's reign resulted in over a million deaths. Hitler's reign killed millions upon millions.

Here are some of the key quatrains relating to these first two Antichrists. Remember, Nostradamus is viewing Napoleon's reign some two hundred years before it occurred, and Hitler's some four hundred years! Yet his accuracy is amazing. This again supports Edgar Cayce's teaching that everything begins in the spirit, takes shape in the mind and then ultimately manifests in the physical. Therefore Nostradamus could see the physical events while they were still in the mental and spiritual dimensions.

Napoleon Bonaparte

An Emperor will be born near Italy
Who will cost his Empire dearly
They will say, "With what people he keeps
   company!"
He is less of a prince than a butcher.

1:60

Napoleon Bonaparte (1769–1821; Emperor 1804–1815) was born on the island of Corsica, very near Italy (line 1). He declared himself emperor, but he was more a war-driven soldier than a prince; butchering men was his greatest skill (line 4). Nostradamus reveals this ruler's nonroyal claim to the throne of France and his war-driven power in the following quatrain:

> Bearing a name which no French King passed on to him
> More fearsome than a thunderbolt
> Tremble will Italy, Spain and England
> Of a strange woman greatly attentive.
>
> 4:54

It is unclear who the strange woman was, perhaps Josephine, though being a traveling soldier, he had many strange women. He also had a strong relationship with his mother. Perhaps she was the attentive strange woman that Nostradamus saw in his dark mirror.

> Pau, Nay, Loron more fire than blood will be
> In praise to swim, the great man will flee to the confluence.
> He will refuse entry to the pies
> And the depraved ones of France will keep them confined.
>
> 8:1

The three names that begin this quatrain are towns in western France, but as we already noted, Nostradamus is playing a word game with us. If one rearranges these letters, one gets "Napaulon Roy." Napaulon is the Corsican spelling of Napoleon! *Roy* means *king*. Interpreters of Nostradamus have pointed out that Napoleon was born under the fire sign, Leo, and because he was not of the royal bloodline, he was truly "more fire than blood." J. H. Brennan points out that "pies" in line 3 "is a colloquial French diminutive of 'magpies,' which, in the original, shares the same spelling as the name *Pius*." This links the verse immediately with two popes, Pius VI and VII, both of whom were actually imprisoned by Napoleon in his capacity as head of what Nostradamus would certainly have considered a "depraved" state (line 4). There is even an explanation of the curious term "confluence" (line 2) in that Pius VI was taken by Napoleon to Valence to die on the confluence of the rivers Rhone and Isere."[3] This is even clearer in the following quatrain:

Roman Pontiff, beware of approaching
A city which is bathed by two rivers
Your blood will be brought up
You and yours when blooms the rose.

2:97

Napoleon had Pius VI and thirty-two of his priests taken to Valence, which is bathed by two rivers. There the pope died, vomiting blood (line 3), on 29 August 1799, the summer season when roses bloom (line 4).

In the following quatrain we have a clear description of this Antichrist:

To the Great Empire [*France*] quite a different
 man comes
Being distant from kindness and happiness
Ruled by one not long from his bed
While the kingdom to great unhappiness.

6:67

History has described Napoleon as a "brooding, lonely, unhappy man (line 2), sometimes strongly influenced by the women who came to his bed (line 3, notably Josephine)."[4] But all the while, the great kingdom of France moves ever closer to disaster and unhappiness (line 4).

The end of Napoleon's reign was seen by Nostradamus this way:

The part of Rome ruled by he who interprets
 the Augur [*i.e., the pope*]
By the French will be much vexed
But the French nation will rue the hour

of the North Wind [*Russia*] and the fleet [*England*] when they drive too far.

2:99

Napoleon drove France and her young men too far, gaining the wrath of Rome, the deadly winter of Russia and the English fleet with her armies. Ultimately the French were defeated and rued the hour that they began following this Antichrist. But history repeats in rhythms and cycles. Europe gives life to another great Antichrist.

Adolf Hitler

In the following quatrains we read Nostradamus's visions of the coming of another Antichrist who would ravage Europe and beyond, leaving a trail of blood, brutality and betrayal. He will begin as all Antichrists, by seducing the populace with what they want to hear. Then he will make them pay dearly for their support.

From the depth of Western Europe
From poor people a child will be born
Who with his tongue will seduce a great crowd
    of people
His fame increases in the Eastern Kingdom.

3:35

Adolf Hitler (1889–1945) was born in Austria, the depths of Western Europe (line 1), to poor parents (line 2). His speeches mesmerized the crowds (line 3). And his reputation increased his relationship with Japan (the Eastern Kingdom of line 4), resulting in the signing of the Tripartite Pact between Germany, Italy and Japan.

Liberty will not be recovered.
It will be occupied by a black, fierce and wicked villain;
When the question of the pontiff is raised
By D'Hister [*Hitler*], the Italian republic will be angry.

5:29

Once allowed a foothold, Hitler and Nazism never stopped their advance, taking liberty and occupying people's lives and lands with a black, fierce wickedness (lines 1 & 2). Also the *Schutzstaffel*, or SS, wore black uniforms and were the elite guard and exterminators for Hitler (line 2). And when the question of the pope was presented to Hitler, he responded "I will go right into the Vatican!" (line 3) And of course, under Mussolini and the Tripartite Pact, Hitler and Mussolini angered many freedom-loving people, including many Italians. (line 4)

Beasts, driven insane with hunger, will cross
the rivers
The greater part of the field will go to Ister
[*Hitler*]
In a cage of iron the great will be dragged away
When the child of Germany observes nothing.

2:24

Hitler's armies and their methods and the subsequent governors who ruled in the wake of their victories were like beasts driven insane with a hunger to possess and purge the world (line 1). In railroad boxcars, many of Europe's great leaders and peoples were dragged away (line 3) by this child of Germany who observed no laws, borders or forms of human decency— nothing (line 4)!

In a spot not too far removed from Venice
The two strongest of Asia [*Japan*] and Africa
[*Italy*]
Will be said to come together with the Rhine
[*Germany*] and Ister [*Hitler*]
Weeping at Malta and the Ligurian coast.

4:68

The Tripartite Axis Pact was signed between Germany, Italy and Japan at the Brenner Pass, not too far from Venice (line 1). Italy annexed Ethiopia, making it the strongest power in Africa (line 2). Malta and Genoa (the Ligurian coast) were both bombarded heavily during the war: Malta by the Axis powers and Genoa by the Allies (line 4).

As Nostradamus prophesied, just as the French would rue the hour they brought Napoleon to power, so the Germans would regret the day they brought Hitler to power. But it is the bane of humanity that we forget, and so a third Antichrist will rise up more terrible than the two who preceded him.

Mabus and Alus

Because this name belongs to one yet to be seen, it is more difficult to identify and interpret the quatrains related to him/her, except where Nostradamus clearly uses the name *Mabus and Alus*, or refers to the Antichrist in a context not fitting Napoleon or Hitler. Erika Cheetham suggests that Mabus and Alus may be "corruptions" of the Latin word *Malus*, which means *evil one*. Nostradamus only mentions these two names once in separate quatrains. Here they are:

Mabus will come, and soon after will die
Of people and beasts a great destruction
Suddenly vengeance will be seen

Blood, hand, thirst, famine when the comet
  passes.

                                    2:62

His last hand through bloody Alus
Will not save him by sea
Between two rivers he will fear the military
  hand
The black and wrathful one makes repentant.

                                    6:33

These quatrains do appear to be very specific.
We can see in them that the Antichrist—bloody,
destructive and vengeful—brings famine and
thirst. We can also see that a comet passing is a
sign of his presence. Somehow hands play a key
role in his activities (line 4 in the first quatrain
and lines 1 and 3 in the second). Erika Cheetham
has proposed that the "military hand" may be the
nuclear "finger on the button" of the 1950s
through the 1990s. In line 3 of the second quatrain the complete annihilation of humanity
(which began between the two rivers of the
Tigris and Euphrates in the Garden of Eden,
where Satan first gained influence) causes even
the Evil One to fear the loss of everything, leaving nothing for him to rule. Line 4 of the second
quatrain—"The black and wrathful one makes
repentant"—is a curious statement. Nostrada-

mus uses the French word *noir* here, which most interpreters translate as *black*. But *noir* also means *dark*. Perhaps this is a reference to the coming day of the Lord, when the sun will not give its light. *Noir* also has a connotation of *evil*. Perhaps it is a reference to the forces of evil and Satan in the context that St. Paul uses in 1 Cor. 5:5: "Hand this man over to Satan, so that the sinful nature may be destroyed and his spirit saved on the day of the Lord." The Lord's day is marked by his wrath on all evil—causing many to repent from their support of the Antichrist influence.

The twentieth century was full of wars. Some of them the likes of which the world has never seen, with more bloodshed than any other period—millions upon millions butchered. Few nations on the earth have avoided some confrontation and bloodshed during this period. As for the passing comet in the Mabus quatrain, it would certainly appear to be Nostradamus's way of dating the coming of this Antichrist, but there are many comets and many have come and gone when the world seemed in great peril.

A Date for the Antichrist

We may have the clearest dating of the coming of the Antichrist (and/or a reference to the two beasts of the Revelation) in these next quatrains:

In the year 1999 and seven months [*July*]
From the sky will come a great King of Terror
To resuscitate the great King of the Mongols
Before and after, Mars reigns happily.

10:72

Certainly this is one of the clearest datings in the whole of Nostradamus's work. It would appear to fit with the prophecies of the Armageddon, a battle fought in the "air" (line 2, "from the sky") between the forces of good and evil.

The resuscitating of the King of the Mongols (line 3) is a terrible thought. History still holds the Mongol hordes and their reign throughout all of Asia and much of Europe during the 1200s as one of the most brutal, cruel, barbarous periods ever. India, Persia, Russia and Eastern Europe all suffered the murderous brutality of these conquerors. When the Mongols defeated the armies of Western Europe, the Vatican and the Holy Land were open to invasion without resistance, and all Christendom appeared to be lost. Then a miracle happened: The great Khan died! To everyone's shock, the Mongol hordes returned home to mourn and fight among themselves, leaving much of the West to rebuild itself.

If we are to assume from this quatrain that these cruel souls are to rise again from the dead to spread their uncaring brutality across the planet, then this is the worst of predictions, suited well to Jesus' statement that lawlessness will reign so freely that the hearts of many will grow cold.[5] However Nostradamus does not clearly say they will assault the world; perhaps a more local event along the lines of China's brutal invasion of Tibet would be enough to fulfill this prophecy.

The Cayce readings support this prophecy, saying that, if the world does not get its act together, then "a hated people will be raised up" among the yellow race. This could be Nostradamus's "resuscitation of the great King of the Mongols."

Nostradamus also foresees the rising of a leader who declares Thursday as his holy day. Islam has Friday, Judaism Saturday, and Christianity Sunday; but this new leader will apparently reform some current religion or develop a new one with Thursday as the holy day. It is not clear if this person is an Antichrist or a good leader, but there are some hints:

From the aquatic triplicity will be born
One who will have Thursday for his holy day
His fame, praise, rule and power will grow
By land and sea to become a tempest to the
  Orient.

1:50

"From the aquatic triplicity" could mean the three water signs of the zodiac: Cancer, Scorpio and Pisces. Perhaps these will be predominant in his horoscope. Or as Henry Roberts suggests,[6] perhaps the aquatic triplicity is the Atlantic, Pacific and Gulf of Mexico—in other words, the U.S.A. with Thanksgiving as its special day, the last Thursday of November. Certainly the U.S. has been giving the Orient (line 4) much attention (China in the early 1900s, Japan in the 40s, Korea in the 50s, Vietnam in the 60s and 70s, Taiwan and again China in the 80s, and again China and North Korea in the 90s). The U.S. has had many ongoing interactions with Asia, good and bad, by land and sea (line 4). In this case then the man in the quatrain could be Franklin D. Roosevelt, who officially declared Thanksgiving Thursday as a U.S. national holiday. This is supported by another quatrain that does appear to foreshadow the founding of the new "fair" land to which many will come and give honor, namely America. This new country begins in the freezing cold winters of Plymouth, Massachusetts, but leads to a Thursday of Thanksgiving.

The land and air will freeze with so much water
When they come to venerate Thursday
That which will be, never was so fair
Of the four quarters they will come to honor him.
10:71

If this is what these quatrains are referring to, then Nostradamus's visions, seen in the mid 1500s, are truly amazing. Nevertheless I'd keep my eye open for someone else declaring Thursday as his holy day. Surprisingly, we have another holy day to watch for:

> The penultimate one of the surname of the Prophet
> Will take Monday for his day of rest
> Wandering far because of his frenzied head
> Delivering a great people from impositions.
>
> 2:28

Penultimate means *next to last*, and a surname is a name held by all members of a family. *The Prophet* is usually a reference to Muhammad, but I don't see how this leads to any conclusions. Perhaps Nostradamus is referring to the prophet who saw the Revelation, St. John, and as we know, the Cayce readings give this prophet a surname, Peniel. This prophet may return, make Monday his day of rest because he works weekends. It's difficult to know exactly what Nostradamus meant. The least we can say is that Nostradamus saw two leaders using Monday and Thursday, respectfully, as their rest day and holy day. All we can do is wait and see how this plays out on the world stage.

There are only two quatrains where the term "Antichrist" is used plainly.

By the Antichrist, three will be quickly
  annihilated
Twenty-seven years of blood will last his war
The heretics dead, captive, exiled
Bloody human corpses, water red, covering
  the earth.

8:77

The chief of London by l'Americh [*American*]
  power
The isle of Scotland burdened with ice [*frost?*]
Roy Reb will have so dreadful an Antichrist
Who will put them all in discord.

10:66

Could the "three" (line 1) of the first quatrain be the same as the three in the second quatrain—namely, London, America and Scotland? Or is Scotland only used as a sign that a major climate change has occurred, putting Scotland under ice and an island separated from the English mainland (line 2)?

Who or what is Roy Reb? *Roy* means *king*, but Reb is unclear. In Judaism, *Reb* is a form of *Rabbi*. Perhaps Nostradamus is speaking of a great deceiver who leads the Jews astray or into discord with one another. However I don't see how this relates to the first two lines of this quatrain. Of course, the twenty-seven-year-long war in the first quatrain could easily relate to the Jews, because they've been in a virtual war since the sixties; and if Nostradamus considers the Islamic opponents to be "heretics" to the teachings of Father Abraham, then his lines about "The heretics dead, captive, exiled [*one of Israel's common punishments*]/Bloody human corpses, water red [*Red Sea?*], covering the earth" has relevance to the Middle Eastern battle that has raged for so long, involving the whole earth in its problems.

Some interpreters say it's Rob Roy of Scotland (1671–1734), a Robin Hood character who rustled cattle and sold his neighbors protection. I don't see how that relates to these quatrains. Erika Cheetham believes the second quatrain relates to U.S. nuclear weapons being housed on Scottish soil with the permission of the chief of London, which caused much discomfort for these three governments, mostly from their own people. Actually I'm inclined to take a broader interpretation of these two quatrains.

The Antichrist is, as Edgar Cayce stated earlier, a spirit, an attitude with chillingly violent, uncaring, unthinking emotions that insidiously creeps into the hearts and minds of individuals, families, communities, nations and leaders, blocking out the light of Christ (which is the love of God and neighbor) and bringing on the conditions necessary for "bloody human corpses, red water and discord" everywhere. Could the "three quickly annihilated" by the Antichrist be "faith, hope and charity?" Could Roy Reb be just that, King Reb or Rebel—that spirit that separates us from a sense of oneness with others and God, allowing us to do whatever seems good to us, with complete disregard for what others might want or need or what the Christ spirit wants? Jesus says the End Times will cause hearts to grow cold; even the elect would fall away if the end time were not shortened. If we consider that Nostradamus used anagrams and wordplay, perhaps the terms Mabus and Alus are simply:

"May-b-us" and "All us"

Is it possible that the Antichrist, no matter who personifies this spirit as a leader, requires us to give it fuel, to give it life in our hearts and minds? Notice in this quatrain how American power makes it happen. America is where the governing influence is by the people, for the people. If that influence becomes tainted with mean-spiritedness, spitefulness, revenge, intolerance, etc., then the Antichrist has gained power.

The power is with the people, each of us, in our hearts and minds. We then give power to families, communities, nations and leaders. What spirit will rule? As God said in Genesis, evil's "desire is for you, but you must master it." Or "Go. Be fruitful and multiply, but subdue the earth" and its influence upon you.

May be us, all of us, have to take hold of our free will and responsibility for our thoughts and actions, and hold others to a high responsibility for their actions and thoughts.

THE PROPHECIES OF HEAVENLY SIGNS

Just as all the End Times prophets have written, Nostradamus also writes that there will be signs in the heavens.

> The great star for seven days will burn
> A cloud will make two suns appear
> The big mastiff will howl all night
> When a great Pope changes his territory.
>
> 2:41

In July 1994, Jupiter, a planet composed of the same gases as our sun, only much cooler, was bombarded with twenty-one comet fragments the size of mountains, causing great clouds of debris to rise from the surface of this huge planet. The comet bombardment went on for six days—a close match to Nostradamus's seven-day prediction (line 1). But what of the two suns and the pope?

The two-suns prophecy is also among the Virgin Mary prophecies, but it does not appear in any of the scriptural or Cayce prophecies, unless the phrase "His star [sometimes "His light"] will be seen in the heavens" is referring to another star or sun appearing in our system. Of course, many interpreters of Nostradamus consider this to be a comet rather than a star or sun. This is probably because it is much easier to conceive of a comet than another sun in our system! But the prophet wrote "two suns." However he did say that the cloud makes it appear as though there are two suns. So perhaps it's an illusion rather than a reality.

The mastiff howling all night is an ominous sign of danger and death since the mastiff is a watchdog. As we shall see in the next section, changes in the papacy are useful signs for timing these quatrains. If the pope moves his abode or even leaves this world (line 4) during or soon after the star burns for seven days, I'd be prepared for the mastiff to howl.

There are quatrains that appear to refer to comets. One of them we have already discussed.

It began with the reference to Mabus and ended with this line: "Blood, hand, thirst, famine, when the comet passes." (2:62) In another quatrain, Nostradamus refers to a "bearded star;" presumably he means a comet (2:15). "In the sky will be seen a fire with a tail of sparks" (2:46) also seems to be describing a comet.

In addition to the bombardment of Jupiter by comet P/Shoemaker-Levy's fragments, some major comets have passed close to the earth since the time of Nostradamus: Nexel in 1720, Kohoutek in 1974, IRAS-Araki-Alcock in 1983, Halley's in 1986, Hyakutake in 1996, and Hale-Bopp in 1997. To Nostradamus and most other religious seekers of the Middle Ages, a comet was always a bad omen, a sign of coming disaster. Actually any heavenly phenomenon is a bad omen because, to them, it portends of "the great and terrible day of the coming of the Lord!" I suppose the star of Bethlehem is one famous example of a heavenly sign of the coming of the Lord. And if you were among the mothers of newborn baby boys in Bethlehem, then the star was a very bad omen as Herod's murdering soldiers descended upon the little town. A great savior had been born to lead the world out of darkness, but the earth suffered much from His coming. Judas thought Jesus would lead an army against Rome, but in A.D. 70, Titus's le-

gions destroyed the great Temple in Jerusalem,
the Jews were scattered, and the Christians were
fed to beasts in the arena and burned at the
stake. There has always been a great conflict between good and evil, light and darkness, since
Michael and Lucifer first battled for control of
heaven. History has recorded well that a major
movement on the part of one always brings a
major countermovement by the other. Jesus receives the Holy Spirit during his baptism with
John, but then is led off into the desert to wrestle
with Satan. A much-quoted Cayce reading says
that wherever you have a channel of light, darkness seeks to enter. Therefore, a heavenly sign
is often a discomforting omen, even if it does
ultimately mean a new era of greater light,
greater good.

There are also several quatrains dealing with
fire in or from the sky:

> Forty-five degrees the sky will be alight
> Fire approaches the great new city
> At once a great flame springs up
> When they wish to see the Normans proven.
>
> 6:97

This last line could be the time indicator.
Therefore we might consider this quatrain to
refer to the D day invasion at Normandy or a

major anniversary celebrating that day ("to see the Normans proven"). It could also be the French people as a whole. Some interpreters believe the forty-five degrees relates to a city along the forty-fifth parallel. With the globe spinning before me, and assuming that the poles are still relatively close to our present situation, the cities I find that lie on or near the forty-fifth parallel are: Portland (OR), Minneapolis, Ottawa, Montreal, Lyon, Milan, Belgrade and Bucharest.

To Nostradamus, viewing this scene in the 1500s, heavy guns (from ships, tanks and artillery) may appear to be firing at forty-five degree angles from the ground, with great fires and explosions resulting. But just to show how terribly difficult it is to understand these quatrains with foresight only, it could refer to fires on the hills surrounding the great new city of San Francisco/Oakland (a mountainside roughly a forty-five degree angle from the flat land) or perhaps the fires around the great new city of Los Angeles, nearer the timing of the fiftieth anniversary of D day? Certainly San Francisco and Los Angeles are very new cities. Of course many believe that this is speaking about a city with the word *new* in its name, i.e., New York.

Brennan believes this quatrain relates to France, a great new city in the land of the Normans,

whose old capital was Rouen on the Seine
River. The great new city could then be Paris
on the Seine, but Paris is a bit above the forty-
fifth parallel, as is Rouen. Perhaps the world is
waiting to see the French prove themselves in
Bosnia, through which runs the forty-fifth parallel? Then the new city would be Sarajevo (but
it's not really new). Or perhaps it refers to
Montreal, a truly new city with French qualities. It is difficult to know until it happens.
Then everyone looks back in hindsight with
amazement.

> By fire from the sky the city is almost razed
> Flooding again threatens Deucalion
> Sardinia vexed by the African fleet
> After Libra leaves Leo.

2:81

Fire from the sky falls upon another unnamed
city. This is also a difficult quatrain to interpret.
In Greek mythology, Deucalion was the only
human left after the great flood (a Noah-like
character). According to this quatrain, even he
will be in danger of not surviving the next one!
Sardinia is an island country to the south of Italy
in the Mediterranean Sea. A Cayce reading refers to Libya as being an earthly reflection of
Libra![7] Could Nostradamus be using this, and

the African fleet is Libya's, or is it the U.S. fleet off the coast of Libya? Or perhaps it is in a future so different from what we presently know that we can't interpret this quatrain without our own vision.

Among the heavenly signs that Nostradamus sees is a "dart of heaven," which we could naturally presume to be a comet or missile.

The dart of heaven will make its journey
Death spoken of, great execution
The stone in the tree, the proud nation brought
  down
Rumor of a human monster, purge and atonement
2:70

J. H. Brennan believes this quatrain fits the Gulf War of Desert Storm rather well. The human monster is Saddam Hussein, whose danger to the U.S. and the Middle East was fed mostly by rumors (line 4). Saddam spoke at great length about the magnitude of death (line 2) that would occur if the U.S. and its Allies attacked, referring to the conflict as the "Mother of All Battles!" But alas, the execution was great (line 2) by the Allies, with their "darts from heaven," and a proud nation, Iraq, was brought down (line 3). I'd also like to point out that this is a nation between the two great rivers of the origin of humanity, the Tigris and Euphrates of the Garden of Eden. Could this be what is meant by "the stone in the tree" which needs purging and atonement for its sins (line 3)? The tree being the Tree of Life, from which we have been banished, and the stone being the tablets of the Ten Commandments through which we will atone and thereby regain the Tree of Life?

Of all Nostradamus's heavenly signs, the clearest are the two suns (2:41) and the Mabus quatrain noting the passing comet as a sign (2:62). Both of these are omens of bad times, vengeance, death, howling and a pope changing his territory.

THE PROPHECIES OF THE POPES

Nostradamus's references to popes is important because it may help us identify the timing of certain events. He seems to be aware of, or his visions give support to, the Irish bishop/ prophet Malachy, who also foresaw history via a line of specifically identified popes.

In 1138, Malachy visited the Vatican. While there, he fell into a deep trance during which he saw the reigning pontiff and the line of succession of 112 popes, followed by the final fall of the Church of Rome. When he awoke, he wrote a complete manuscript on the vision, giving each pope a Latin motto. The manuscript was sent to the Vatican after Malachy's passing, where it was stored in secret archives until 1590, long after Nostradamus's death. Later, around 1730–40, a monk called "The Monk of Padua" wrote a manuscript listing a sequence of popes and the ultimate end of the papacy that closely followed Malachy's, also using Malachy's mottoes for the popes.

In the twentieth century, Malachy calls Benedict XV *Religio Depopulata*, which could relate to his being the pope during WWI, certainly a period of "depopulation of religion." Pius XII (1939–1958), Malachy called *Pastor Angelicus*, referring to his angelic shepherding of the Church. Many followers considered him extremely "saintly." He was followed by John XXIII (1958–63), called *Pastor et Nauta* (shepherd and navigator), perhaps referring to his position as Archbishop of Venice or his reconvening of the Ecumenical Council for the first time since 1869. The council used the symbols of a cross and a ship, perhaps indicative of the shepherd and navigator. After him came, *Flos Florum* (Flower of Flowers), Paul VI (1963–78). His coat of arms contained a floral design. After him came *De Mediatate Lunae* (the middle or half of the moon), John Paul I (26 August 1978–28 September 1978).

This is one of the shortest and most suspicious papal reigns. John Paul I was only sixty-six and in good health when he suddenly died. He had disturbed his Curia (Senate of Cardinals) by stating in one of his earliest speeches that God was not only the Heavenly Father but also the Heavenly Mother. He began to openly support women's rights and agreed to meet with a U.S. Congressional delegation to discuss artificial birth control! Just prior to his curious death, he asked his Secretary of State, Cardinal Jean Villot, to begin an investigation of the Vatican Bank and secret memberships of his priests in the Freemason's Lodge P2. The next morning he was dead. Investigators were surprised that Cardinal Villot initially gave them false information during their questioning and that the cardinals quickly embalmed the body, then cremated it, against strict Catholic custom at that time. Stranger still, Cardinal Villot died within six months of these events.[8] Here's what Nostradamus wrote four hundred years earlier:

When the sepulchre of the great Roman is
   found
The day after will be elected a Pope
By his Senate he will not be approved
Poisoned is his blood by the sacred chalice.

3:65

He who will have government of the Great
Cape [*the pope*]
Will be led to take action
The twelve Red Ones [*cardinals*] will come to
spoil the cover
Under murder, murder will come to be done.

4:11

If this is ever found to be the case, the scandal
will rock the papacy to its foundations, perhaps
changing it forever. Could Nostradamus be referring to this in the next quatrain:

In the sacred temples, there will be made
scandals
They will be thought of as honors and praise-
worthy matters
By one who they mark for silver, gold and coins
The end will be torments very strange.

9:6

If banking, murder and Mafia-connection
scandals do surface in the Vatican, it could be
said that Daniel's "abomination of desolation
standing where it ought not to be" may be coming true before our eyes. These types of scandals
in all religions and denominations are being
seen more and more, causing Daniel's abomination of desolation to come to life in a place
where it ought not to be. We've seen leaders

of massive congregations go down in flaming
scandals of moral and financial corruption. Perhaps there will come a day when the sacred
temples will be desolate of true spiritual and
moral light.

After John Paul I, comes *De Labore Solis* (the
labor of the sun), John Paul II, Karol Wojtyla
from Poland. J. H. Brennan points out that the
part of Poland from which John Paul II came was
originally a portion of ancient France. Therefore
the following quatrain may refer to him:

Not from Spain, but from ancient France
He will be elected from the trembling ship
To the enemy he will make assurance
Who in his reign will be a cruel blight.

5:49

Brennan considers the trembling ship to be
the Church itself. The great enemy of Polish
John Paul II would be none other than the former Soviet Union. John Paul II made assurances
(line 3) to the Soviets concerning the strikes in
Poland by the workers, assurances that may
have kept them from doing what they did in
Hungary and Czechoslovakia. It is said that
John Paul II sent a message to Moscow that, if
they mounted an invasion against Poland, he
would fly to Warsaw and stand, in full papal

regalia, before the approaching tanks. Brennan goes on to say that though John Paul II was successful in this situation, the Soviet blight (line 4) continued through much of his early years as pope. Then came the assassination attempt, the first one. But the second, which received little press, caught more of Nostradamus's attention:

> Oh great Rome, your ruin comes close
> Not of your walls, but of your blood and substance
> The sharp one of letters will be so horrible a notch
> Pointed steel placed up his sleeve, ready to wound.

> 10:65

Mehmet Ali Agca was the Turk who shot John Paul II. It was believed that the KGB was behind the shooting. But the stabber was an educated priest who, during a papal visit to Portugal in 1982, pulled a long knife from out of his sleeve and attempted to kill John Paul II. This attempt did not receive much press. But Nostradamus certainly seems to be viewing this event, noting perhaps the failure: "your ruin comes close."

After John Paul II, the current pope, Malachy and the Monk of Padua predict only two more: *Gloria Olivae* (glory of the olive), whom the

Monk of Padua says will take the name Leo XIV, and *Petrus Romanus* (Peter of Rome). Malachy predicts that Peter of Rome will be the last pope, and that the city will be burned. The Monk of Padua also predicts the burning of the city when the last pope sits on the throne. When is the end? If the present pope continues for another few years, then give *Gloria Olivae* about ten years. Peter of Rome would very likely take the throne in the early years of the twenty-first century.

> The great star for seven days will burn
> A cloud will make two suns appear
> The big mastiff will howl all night
> When a great Pope changes his territory.

2:41

It may be by war or scandal that the pope has to change his territory. Whatever the cause, when we see a pope changing his territory, I'd look for this quatrain's dark omen to begin.

PROPHECIES OF EARTH CHANGES

Are the prophecies of war and bloodshed, disease and pestilence, famine, drought, flood and earthquake prophecies about this century? Here are two quatrains that make one think so:

> After the great human misery, an even greater
>   approaches
> *The great motor of the cycles* [or centuries] *renews*
>   [the year 2000?]
> Rain, blood, milk, famine, sword and pestilence
> In the sky will be seen a fire with a tail of sparks
>   [*a comet?*].
>
> 2:46 [my italics]

> Saturn and a water sign in Sagittarius
> In its highest increase of exaltation
> Pestilence, famine, death from military hand
> *The century approaches its renewal.* [the year
>   2000?]
>
> 1:16 [my italics]

The first quatrain seems to be referring to the renewal of cycles of the centuries, or a millennium, when the centuries start over. The second one is clearly referring to the millennium. Since he was prophesying in the 1500s, we can assume he wasn't referring back to A.D. 999; therefore it is likely he is referring to A.D. 2000. However I want to share with you that, in a letter to his son, Nostradamus clearly says that his prophecies are from "his time to the year A.D. 3797." His End Times prophecies could even relate to

A.D. 3000. Being finite persons, we tend to see our age as the age.

The millennium hysteria caused near panic in A.D. 999. Christendom holds closely to the belief that the end of the world will be at the end of a thousand-year period, a millennium, so each millennium is met with high anxiety and expectations. Certainly this was true for the year 2000, with widespread concerns of Y2K computer failures and other issues, and will be as well when we approach the third millenium. However the scriptural prophecies state that the End Times will be followed by a thousand-year period of peace when the Messiah will reign and Satan will be bound.[9] Therefore Nostradamus's 3797 could include the final thousand years of peace, bringing us back to a period from 1797 through 2797 for the thousand-year battle of Armageddon (Cayce states that the battle will last for a thousand years[10]), which ends with the reign of the Messiah for another thousand years. This would put A.D. 2000 as a major but not a climactic millennium mark. Significant changes may well occur, physically and spiritually, but the passing of earth and heaven, as Jesus spoke of it,[11] is not yet. A last point about the second quatrain. Pluto, a planet not yet discovered in Nostradamus's time is the ruler of the water sign Scorpio. Currently it is in Sagittarius and during the course of 2001 it entered into a tension producing relationship to Saturn.

As with all the End Times and earth-change prophecies, earthquakes and floods top the list of predicted events; great fires appear, major cities are lost, and a pole shifts, though this isn't as clear in Nostradamus's writings as it is in Cayce's. Here are some of the quatrains that appear to predict earth changes:

Near Auch, Lectoure and Mirande
A great fire will fall from the sky for three
    nights
A thing will happen stupendous and miraculous
And shortly after the ground will tremble.

1:46

Some interpreters believe this quatrain refers to a comet falling to earth, followed by earthquakes. Others believe it refers to our first true visitation by aliens in ships that appear as fires in the night, their landing causing the whole ground to shake. The thing that strikes me from this quatrain is the mention of the city of Auch, the capital of ancient Gascony, which included the Pyrenees Mountains. The Cayce readings clearly identify a major cycle beginning in ancient Egypt and continuing to the Pyrenees Mountains, then on to the year 1998. Cayce's teaching that a new body will appear, referencing St. Paul's comment about us all being changed,[12] could be the "thing will happen stupendous and miraculous" (line 3).

> They will think to have seen the sun at night
> When the pig, half a man is seen
> Noise, chants, battles which appear fought in
>   the sky
> And brute beasts will be heard to speak.
>
> 1:64

This is a strange one. It seems to be about an extremely bright light at night, with battles fought in the sky and a pig that is half man, with animals speaking. Animals speaking could be Nostradamus's viewing of our work with dolphins, chimpanzees and selected birds. The pig that is half man is seen by Erika Cheetham as a modern-day jet pilot in his oxygen mask, helmet, goggles and flight suit, fighting a battle in the air—which Nostradamus would have seen as very strange. In fact, a battle of this nature may also appear as bright as daylight though it was being fought at night. Jets and bombs make tremendous noise and strange sounds; perhaps rockets and missiles sound like droning chants until they strike (line 3). Ms. Cheetham could be right about this one. If so, it is only a view into our times by a sixteenth-century man, having nothing to do with earth changes per se.

> The great famine which I see approaching
> Turning one way and then another, then becom-
> ing universal
> So great and long that they will pluck
> The roots from the wood and the child from
> the breast.
>
> 1:67

Has the world already seen much of this famine? Is it the worldwide Great Depression of the 1930s? Or is it still winding its way across the planet, ultimately coming to all nations and lands? The last line of this quatrain is reminiscent of Jesus saying "woe to those who nurse babies" during the End Times.[13] As I view the African famines on television, those nursing mothers seem sorrowfully helpless, their bodies unable to produce even the basic nourishment for their babies.

> Ennosigee [*earth-shaking*] fire from the center of
> the earth
> Will make trembling all around the New City
> Two great rocks will long war against each
> other

Then Arethusa will color red the new river.

1:87

Two great rocks warring against each other would be an excellent description of tectonic plates, just as we see in the Western portion of America, particularly California, and in Japan. Since Nostradamus precedes this tectonic war with "fire from the center of the earth," I'm inclined to look for volcanic activity to precede the quake and the trembling of the New City. In his time, Paris, London and Rome were great cities, so it must be one of the newer cities on a tectonic plate, perhaps Los Angeles, San Francisco, San Diego, Tokyo (which would be a new city for Nostradamus) or even New York, though New York's fault has not been warring as long a time as L.A.'s has. This quatrain seems to fit California's cities better than any others.

The name *Arethusa* (line 4) is from Greek mythology. Arethusa was a woodland nymph and one of the attendants of Artemis (goddess of the moon, Apollo's twin sister). Alpheus, a river god, saw her bathing in a stream and tried to embrace her. As she fled under the sea, she called on Artemis for help and was changed into a fountain. It was believed that Alpheus, in the form of a river, flowed underground to Sicily, where he was united with her in the fountain of Arethusa in the city of Syracuse. There is also an orchid/herb called Dragon's mouth, its botanical name *Arethusa bulbosa*. Known also as swamp pink, it grows in swamps and bogs from Newfoundland south to North Carolina and west to Minnesota. Could the "new river" that Arethusa colors red be in these areas? If it is the Midwest of the U.S., then this could be the same prophecy as Cayce's—the Great Lakes will empty into the Gulf of Mexico, turning the Mississippi red with blood of victims? Then the "new city" on the forty-fifth parallel could be from Minneapolis to Montreal. The Dragon's mouth may well be a reference to increased volcanic activity that precedes the new river's movement. Again it's difficult to know.

TERRORISM AND NOSTRADAMUS

Immediately following the terrible terrorist attack on the United States on 11 September 2001, rumors spread that Nostradamus had actually written quatrains prophesying this event. But as cooler heads began to review Nostradamus's writings, no such specific quatrains could be found. Here are two of the quatrains that people are quoting. As is often the case with Nostradamus's work, neither of these clearly correlates with the details of this terrorist event.

This quatrain is being misquoted to fit the situation by changing 1999 to "turn of the century." But it clearly states the year and month as follows:

> In the year 1999 and seven months
> From the sky will come a great King of Terror
> To resuscitate the great King of the Mongols
> Before and after, Mars reigns happily.

> 10:72

Let's assume that Nostradamus missed this date by a few years because humanity is making changes in its destiny. He indeed used the word *terror* and identified someone as the *King of Terror*, which would fit Osama bin Laden and his band of terrorists. Mars, the god of war, would certainly be ruling happily during these times. Astrologically the planet Mars spent six long months in the sign of Sagittarius, an unusual event, perhaps even a "long reign," just before the terrorist attack. During and after the attack, however, it spent the more normal amount of time, seven weeks, in the next sign of Capricorn. But how does this quatrain relate to resuscitating the King of the Mongols? Could Nostradamus, viewing from his sixteenth-century perspective, mistake the Afghans for Mongols? From sixteenth-century France, Afghanistan would certainly appear to be in the land of the Mongol hordes who overran Eastern Europe, Russia and the Holy Lands in the twelfth century. Or could he simply be using poetic license in creating an analogy of the terrible scourge of the Mongols upon his people with the coming scourge of terrorists upon ours? It is all possible, but it requires some stretching of the words in the original text.

Here is the other quatrain that people are circulating:

> Forty-five degrees the sky will burn
> Fire approaches the grand new city
> Instantly a grand flame springs up
> When they wish to see the Normans proven.

> 6:97

As we said earlier in this chapter, this quatrain may be translated as relating to an event at forty-five degrees latitude, but nothing related to this event corresponds to this location. New York City is not on the forty-fifth parallel. It is on the fortieth. We might consider that something is moving at a forty-five-degree angle, but nothing corresponds with that either. The jets that struck the Towers were more likely at ninety-degree angles to the buildings. Bosnia is on the forty-fifth parallel, and as we concluded earlier, it is a better fit for this quatrain, especially with our accidental bombing of the Chinese embassy in Bosnia (Chinese being much closer to twelfth-century Mongols than anyone else). However the "Normans" is clearly a reference that can be correlated to the New York attack, given that the Normans began the Crusades against the Muslims, and Osama bin Laden refers in his pronouncements to *Saladin*, the Muslim victor over the Crusaders. His terrorist actions over the past several years have tested or "proven" the "Normans." The "great new city" may correlate to New York City, but there have been many great new cities from the time of Nostradamus. Bosnia may or may not be one of them.

Wars, disasters and terrors figure prominently throughout Nostradamus's writings and may relate to many events that have happened from his time. However, of all of Nostradamus's writings, his forecast of changes in the papal leadership are the most easily corroborated, and they can be correlated with prophesies from Malachy and the Monk of Padua, as we have seen in this chapter. If the succession of popes occurs as foretold, then we can expect the other prophecies to be fulfilled as well, indicating that the coming of the new age and the ending of our times has begun. After this current pope, there should be only two more. If the next one has any connection with the Jews and takes the name of Leo, then truly the future can be known and predicted. We will see.

Nostradamus's Long-term Vision

Critics of Nostradamus's work say that almost anything can be predicted using his quatrains because they are so open to interpretation. I've tried to select those that have some specificity to them.

I'll close this chapter with one of his quatrains that indicates how, in some distant future, life on this planet as we know it, will go on:

Twenty years of the moon's reign pass
Seven thousand years another monarch shall hold
When the sun takes up his days
Then shall my prophecies be complete.

1:48

Seven thousand years is a long time. I believe we have many more adventures to enjoy and make the most of before the final end comes. What we are approaching now is a great change from one era to another. It may be challenging and transforming, but as Jesus said, it is only the birth pains of the delivery of a new age of hope and peace.

4

THE PROPHECIES OF THE HOLY MOTHER

THE DIVINE FEMININE SPEAKS

There have been hundreds of reported appearances of the Virgin Mary. *Apparition* has become the word used to describe these visions, a word that means *to unexpectedly appear, to become visible without warning or preparation*. It also refers to a phantom or ghost. Everyone that has reported seeing the image agrees that it is not physical, it is surrounded by light, sound and movement that is not normal, and it appears without warning or invitation. The seers are usually engaged in everyday activities when suddenly she appears. Lightning or a clap of thunder sometimes accompanies her appearance. In some cases, the appearance of a male "light-being," or angel, precedes her. Sometimes the angel has identified himself as the archangel Michael, whom we know as the archangel of the heavenly battle against Lucifer. The female image identifies herself in different ways, calling herself at different times: The Lady of Peace, The Queen of Peace, The Immaculate Heart; to the children in Rwanda, Africa, she called herself "The Mother of the World," which appears to be a clear reference to Genesis's name for Eve, "The Mother of All."

There are some consistent features to these apparitions. She is always bright with light, a veil over her head, wearing a seamless dress (often white, once blue), barefoot, and able to move without walking—most describe her movement as "gliding." She is always suspended above the ground, and appears and disappears with great speed. As mentioned earlier, lightning and/or thunder or some unusual sound with light usually accompanies her appearance. Colors frequently associated with her appearances are starlight white and sky blue.

Her appearance and language have a universal quality to them. The black children to whom she appeared in Africa could not recall what "color" her skin was. They described her as being "like them," but not black, white or "half-caste." To the white girls in Medjugorje, Yugoslavia, her skin color was not discernible, except that she was not white like her pictures, nor was she any other color. She spoke in the native language of each group that saw her (Tolpetlac, Spanish, French, Portuguese, Slavic, Rwandan, English, and so on).

Overall, her teachings are universal in their tone and content, supporting no specific faith or doctrine. For example, to the children in Medjugorje she said, "There is only one God and one Faith." To the children in Rwanda she said, "Before God there is neither Protestant nor Catholic, nor Adventist, nor Muslim, nor any branch of other creeds. The true son of God is whoever does God's will." A Catholic priest in the Rwandan school where the apparitions occurred notes that "the Lady" never asked the Protestant or Muslim pupils to "become Catholic, but to recognize her as the Mother of God."

A peculiar and fascinating fact about these apparitions is the progression of the time of day that she appeared—beginning before dawn in the Guadalupe apparition in 1531, morning in Lourdes in 1858, noon in Fatima in 1917, evening in Medjugorje in 1981 and the nightfall appearances later that same year in Rwanda. This progression fits well with ancient mystical teachings that the progression of the sun through the heavens reflects the progression of humanity through the earth.

The earliest of her apparitions that I could find was to the disciple James in Saragossa, Spain, in A.D. 40, instructing him to build a church there. In 1251, she appeared to Simon Stock (later St. Simon) at Aylesford, Kent. In this apparition she identified herself as "Our Lady of Mt. Carmel," a name the archangel Michael also used for her during the apparitions at Garabandal in 1961. Mt. Carmel was the ancient site of the Essene Temple (a sect of the Jewish faith at the time of Christ), where, according to the Cayce readings, women served as high priests. This, of course, would mean that women went into the most sacred place in the Temple, the Holy of Holies, and experienced direct contact with God, returning to give a message to the waiting people. To my knowledge, during this time in history, women were not allowed to enter the Holy of Holies in any of the other Hebrew sects. I don't believe any are doing so today. The Essenes had a rare sense of the Divine Feminine and its representation in woman. The Cayce readings also say that Mary, the mother of Jesus, was trained and chosen at the Temple in Mt. Carmel.

She appears again in 1475 at Bétharram and

1510 at Garaison, both in the Pyrenees Mountains. This is the first of a long and important series of apparitions in the Pyrenees. Note how significant this is when we consider Cayce's teaching that the great path we have been walking has led from the ancient lands of Atlantis and Egypt to the Death of the Son of Man as a man, then to the Pyrenees, and finally to 1998 (see the Cayce section in this book for details).

Let's focus our attention on the major apparitions, dating from 1531 to 2000: Guadalupe, Lourdes, Fatima, Garabandal, Zeitoun, Medjugorje, Rwanda and Assiut.

GUADALUPE, MEXICO, 1531

The Virgin Mary's most profound and well-known appearances began at the same time as Nostradamus was divining his quatrains, but far away from France, in Guadalupe, Mexico, in 1531. She appeared to a native South American Indian. His Indian name in English was He-who-speaks-like-an-eagle. He and his wife paid taxes to the Aztec governors, but loved the Spanish friars who spoke of one god who was loving, like a father. He and his wife eventually became Christians and changed their names to Juan Diego and Maria Lucia. One hard winter

Maria became ill and died. Juan was sad, but believed that Maria was now in heaven with the loving Father. He continued to go to church every Saturday and Sunday.

On 9 December 1531, before dawn, Juan set out for his usual Saturday church devotionals. He was wearing his native Indian clothing, which included a *tilma,* a coarse-woven cape made from cactus fiber. As he approached the hill of Tepeyac, he heard what he thought was a choir of birds chanting like the friars. Looking up, he saw a brilliant white cloud upon the hilltop. As he approached the cloud it expanded into a rainbow of color, the chanting stopped, and an exciting silence surrounded the area. Speaking in his own native tongue, a female voice called his name, "Juan, Juan Diego." Without a moment's thought he ran to the top of the hill, the cloud parted and he saw a beautiful lady in the robes of an Aztec princess. The lady was so brilliant that Juan thought she was standing in front of the sun but it was before dawn. "Juan, smallest and most believed of my sons," spoke the lady. "Where are you off to, Juanito?" He told her that he was on his way to a special High Mass in honor of the Mother of God. The glowing lady countered, "My dear son, I am the Mother of God, and I want you to listen carefully. I have an important message to give you.

Go to the bishop of Mexico and tell him that I have sent you. Tell him to build a church here because I want to show my love to your people. Tell him all that you have seen."

As one might expect, it was not only difficult to get in to see the bishop—it was also difficult to convince him of the message and the need to build another church in this faraway land. However, the bishop was not completely resistant to the Indian's story and request, for he instructed Juan to return again another time and repeat the entire story to him. But it had never occurred to Juan that his message would not be received and acted upon immediately. He was in despair as he trudged by the hill of Tepeyac on his way home. To his amazement, the glowing lady was still there! He climbed the hill and said, "Dear lady, I have failed." He told her every detail of his journey and meeting with the bishop. He closed his story by suggesting that it would be better if she sent a nobleman or a child rather than a poor Indian farmer. She responded, "I have many messengers I could send, but it is you I need and want for this purpose. Go back to the bishop tomorrow and tell him that I demand he build a church here."

As we might expect, the bishop demanded a sign to prove that she was indeed the Mother of God. Therefore, to prove her authenticity to the bishop, she imbued Diego's cape with her image. This portrait is still above the altar in the Church of Our Lady of Guadalupe. The fabric of the cape has not aged or changed for more than four hundred years, even though the cape has been unprotected for much of this time. The paint, if that is what it is, cannot be associated with any that is known.

As far as we know, the glowing lady, "Mother of God," did not prophesy any future events to Juan Diego, except the conversion of his people and her love coming upon them. Furthermore, no one really knows what Guadalupe means. The Lady simply called herself "The Lady of Guadalupe," and so the church became known by this name, but no town or person had ever used the name before. Some researchers have pointed out that the word does have meaning in Arabic—it means: *hidden river*. But why she would use an Arabic word is unclear.

After Guadalupe, she appears occasionally, but during the 1800s and the 1900s the frequency and intensity increase dramatically.

In 1830, a vision of the Virgin Mary appeared to Catherine Labouré, a nun in a convent in Paris. To Catherine, she prophesied the imminent overthrow of the French throne, very in keeping with Nostradamus's prophecy of this event. She also told Catherine of events that would occur over the next forty years. It is claimed that Catherine's body, like Bernadette's of Lourdes, has remained uncorrupted to this day.

LOURDES, FRANCE, 1858

In 1846, an apparition of the Virgin Mary was reported in LaSalette, France, by a young shepherdess, Agnes de Sagazan, mostly requesting a church be built. But in 1858, one of the greatest and longest-running apparitions occurred in Lourdes, France (continuing the Pyrenees apparitions).

We must remember the times in which these apparitions occurred. In 1793, the French Revolution actually outlawed religion. The parish church in Lourdes had been turned into a gunpowder factory. In the early 1800s, the law was amended and religion was allowed. In 1855, a cholera epidemic broke out in Lourdes and killed many. In 1857–1858, famine killed many more in Lourdes. These were very, very hard times.

In the early morning, a fourteen-year-old girl, poor and ill, named Bernadette, was searching among stones and brush for firewood and bones to sell to the rag-and-bone man. She was looking along the riverbank when she noticed a glow coming from a small cave in the hillside. The glow was above a rosebush. As she looked closer at this strange sight, she saw a beautiful girl dressed in white appear. The girl beckoned her to come closer. Bernadette froze in fright and began saying her rosary. The image disappeared. Bernadette told her sister and mother what had happened. Life had been very hard for her mother, and now she believed her eldest daughter was hallucinating! The mother beat Bernadette for "telling stories," and then her sister, too, just to get the point across. The children were forbidden to go near the cave by the river.

Two days later, Bernadette, driven by some inner urge, told her local priest about the whole experience. The priest got her permission to tell the parish priest, Father Peyramale, and the following Sunday, Bernadette received permission to revisit the grotto. Seven girls with holy water approached the cave; Bernadette entered and knelt and prayed. The glowing girl appeared, but only Bernadette could see her. Suddenly, another friend rolled a large stone down the hill from above the cave. The stone landed very close to the cave with a loud crash. Bernadette didn't flinch, remaining entranced. The other girls panicked and ran for help. Finding the local miller, they returned with him to find Bernadette still in a trance. He picked her up and carried her back to his mill. Despite his attempts to distract her, she stayed in a focused gaze with a smile on her face. Eventually, she returned to normal and told everyone what she had seen.

As with so many of the seers of these apparitions, Bernadette was immediately ridiculed and berated. However, some of the townspeople thought Bernadette was truly seeing someone, but it must be, they surmised, the disincarnate soul of a pious girl who had died the year before rather than the Virgin Mary. One of the prominent women of the town arranged to take Bernadette back to the grotto to observe her and the surroundings during these visions. She put pen and paper in Bernadette's hands and told her to ask the name of the glowing girl and then write it down. Bernadette entered the cave, knelt and prayed. Shortly thereafter, she went into ecstasy. When it was over, Bernadette told them the glowing girl said "it was not necessary to know her name." This was the first time the apparition had spoken, and she spoke in a Pyrenean dialect, Bigourdan, which Bernadette knew well, but the prominent lady considered it to be a crude language of the country peasants.

The glowing girl also asked Bernadette to come to the grotto for the next fifteen days, saying, "I don't promise to make you happy in this world, but in the next." During one of these apparitions, Bernadette was observed to be holding a lighted candle while in ecstasy. The candle burned down so low that the flame was actually inside her cupped hands! Yet when the ecstasy was over, she was found to have suffered no burns. On another occasion, after being in a trance during an apparition, Bernadette hugged a sickly child of the town on her way home, and the child became well—for a time. Within the grotto Bernadette was also guided to uncover a healing spring. Unfortunately, when she emerged from her discovery, she was covered with dirt, which the judging crowd saw as demeaning and ridiculous—never realizing how miraculous that spring would prove to pilgrims in the future.

The real story of Lourdes is in its ongoing magic. To date, there have been nearly four thousand reported cures at this grotto/spring, of which the medical community formally recognizes nearly two hundred as inexplicable cures of known illnesses. One of the earliest and most renowned cures was the healing of the two-year-old son of Napoleon III.

From February 18th to March 4th, Bernadette saw the glowing girl thirteen times, for a total of eighteen appearances in all. As far as the prophetic aspect of the apparitions at Lourdes, Bernadette says the glowing girl, who eventually identified herself as "The Immaculate Conception," told her "secrets" of things to come and what she (the glowing girl) was going to do. Little, however, is known about the content of these secrets.

FATIMA, PORTUGAL, 1917

"A strong wind began to shake the trees," recalls Lucy, who was nine years old when this happened. "Then we began to see in the distance, above the trees that stretched to the east, a light whiter than snow in the form of a young man, quite transparent and as brilliant as crystal." She and her companions, eight-year-old Francisco and six-year-old Jacinta, watched in wonder as the light-being approached them. It said to them, "Do not be afraid. I am the Angel of Peace. Pray with me." They knelt beside him on the bare spot of dirt next to a large white stone and repeated after him, "My God, I believe, I adore, I hope, and I love You. I ask forgiveness for those who do not believe, nor adore, nor hope, nor love You." Then he was gone.

They returned to their village but told no one of their experience. The young man's coming had left them with a strange feeling of heaviness and portent. In their hearts they wondered and continued that strange prayer.

Later in the summer, the young man came again, this time to Lucy's backyard. He said, "What are you doing? You must pray! Pray!" Then he explained to the children that their prayers could bring peace to Portugal. Lucy, Francisco and Jacinta prayed every day with great intensity and devotion. That fall he came again. This time he came with the Holy Grail, the Chalice of Communion, which he left suspended in midair as he knelt with them again to pray. Rising from prayer, the light-being gave the Communion Host to Lucy, as the body of Christ, and the Chalice to Jacinta and Francisco, as the blood of Christ. As he did this, he said, "Take and drink the body and blood of Jesus Christ, horribly outraged by ungrateful men. Repair their crimes and console your God."

When the angel had gone, there was only silence. None of them spoke. Sealed in this special moment, they simply sat together in the quiet.

But life goes on, and eventually the children returned to their normal routines of school, play and chores. The following spring, on 13 May 1917 to be exact, they were tending sheep in the pasture, nearly a mile and a half from home, when the young man returned, but with a twist.

At noon, from out of a clear blue sky came

what appeared to be two flashes of lightning. It startled the children. They turned in unison, and above a small holm oak was the figure of a young lady, about sixteen years old, all alight, glowing with a sparkling radiance. It appeared that a star was actually wrapped in the folds of her dress. At first the light seemed too brilliant to look into for long, but the children adjusted to the radiance, and gradually more details of the lady were visible. She was wearing a white mantle with gold edges over her head. Her dress was blue, like the sky. When Lucy asked who she was, she simply answered "I have come from heaven." She told the children that she would tell them exactly who she was on October 13th; until then they were to come to this spot on the thirteenth of each month and pray. Then she asked, "Will you offer yourselves to God and bear all the sufferings He sends you, in atonement for the sins that offend Him and for the conversion of sinners?" The children enthusiastically responded, "Oh, we will! We will!" "Then," she said, "you will have a great deal to suffer, but the grace of God will be with you and will strengthen you. Say the rosary every day to bring peace to the world and an end to war." In a blaze of light, the lady disappeared to the east.

Little Jacinta could not keep silent any longer.

The light man, or angel, always filled her with a heavy sense of omen, or something powerful coming. But the light lady filled her with happiness and life. After supper that night, Jacinta told her mother. Little did Jacinta know how the adult world was going to react. Her parents spoke with Francisco's parents, and they all spoke with the parents of the eldest child, Lucy. Lucy's mother was furious and horrified. She believed her daughter had created a terrible hoax, and the whole village would know about it! She beat, begged and ordered her daughter to recant this disgraceful lie. These were hard times for the children. Reality had raised its powerful head, and there was no room for beings from heaven.

Finally, a month had passed and it was time to return to the site on the thirteenth of June. The children's parents would not go with them, but some of the villagers came along. To everyone's surprise, the lightning flashed in the midst of the noonday sun and the light lady appeared above the little holm oak. She spoke to the children, saying, "I want you to continue saying the rosary every day. And after each one of the mysteries, my children, I want you to pray in this way: 'O my Jesus, forgive us and deliver us from the fire of hell. Take all souls to heaven, especially those in greatest need.' " Lucy, perhaps weary of the earth's harsh reaction to her claims of heavenly visions, asked the Lady, "Will you take us to heaven?" Surprisingly, the Lady answered, "Yes. I will take Jacinta and Francisco soon, but you will remain a little longer, since Jesus wishes you to make me known and loved on earth. He wishes also for you to establish devotion in the world to my Immaculate Heart."

The crowd who knelt around the children saw the lightning, but not the apparition. However, they could hear a small voice speaking in response to Lucy's comments and questions, but could not make out what it was saying. Above the tree, they saw only a little cloud. When Lucy said the Lady was leaving, the crowd saw the little cloud rise very slowly and move off to the east. This, however, was enough phenomena to make the children celebrities. Unfortunately, to some people, they were notorious celebrities of the ridiculous! Strangers and neighbors began to ridicule and taunt the children. People in authority questioned them over and over for every weary detail, looking for the flaw in their stories. Lucy's mother and the local priest had almost convinced Lucy that she had been duped by the devil! The little girl was in torment over the whole thing. It was as the light lady had foretold, the children suffered much for what they had seen. Lucy had actually decided not to go on the thirteenth of the next month.

On July 13th, the village of Fatima was shocked when hundreds of seekers from all over came to their village to join with the children in the vigil for the Lady of Light. It was a hot summer day. The sun was blinding. However, at noon, the sun paled, though the sky was cloudless and blue. Silence swept through the crowds as they began to hear "a little buzzing sound." Many saw a little ball of light settle above the tiny holm oak. But the sight of the Lady and the sound of her voice were only seen and heard by the children. Not surprisingly, Lucy came at the last minute, driven by something inside her, despite all the terrible repercussions that were sure to follow.

The Lady repeated her request for prayer to end war and bring peace to the world, and promised that she would reveal her identity on October 13th. She gave another prayer, "O Jesus, this is for the love of thee, for the conversion of sinners, and in reparation for sins committed against the Immaculate Heart of Mary." Then she told the children a threefold secret. This was followed by a view into the nature of hell, which the Lady sadly said is "where the souls of sinners go. It is to save them that God wants to establish in the world devotion to my Immaculate Heart. If you do what I tell you, many souls will be saved, and there will be peace." Then followed a prophecy of the fate of humanity and nations from 1917 into the future. With a clap of thunder the vision was over.

The crowd pressed in upon the children, some seeking to touch their garments, some to spit into their little faces and mock them. The cruelty of the unbelievers was surprising. Lucy's mother beat her with a broomstick. Every woman in the village deemed it their duty to slap sense into these crazy, troublemaking children. These little ones could go nowhere without physical and emotional abuse and torment.

On September 13th, the children were much weary of the world's oppressive reaction to their visions of heaven and light-beings. They had suffered at the hands of cruel, condemning people, even among their own loved ones. When the Lady appeared that month, Lucy began with this pleading request, "So many believe that I am an impostor and a cheat that they say I deserve to be hanged and burned. Will you please perform a miracle so that all of them can believe?" Just as Jesus was always asked to show the doubters a sign, so little Lucy was now asking the Lady to show her a sign. When the Lady agreed to show all a sign on October 13th, the children proclaimed it openly, believing that everyone would begin to act differently. To their surprise, the ridicule and abuse increased. As the date approached, the newspapers were printing satirical stories about "the three little deceivers." Freemason groups and civic groups threatened to bomb the children's homes. In the night, Lucy's distraught mother would wake her from sleep, shaking her and demanding that she confess her fantasy before it was too late.

Finally, October 13th arrived. Seventy thousand people crammed into the pasture to witness the event! Some came to see the farce, others to witness a miracle from God. It was bitter cold. Rain fell all night and into the day. Thousands of black umbrellas created an eerie scene across the pasture. Many prayed and chanted. The rain grew intense. Gray, wet and cold was the aura of that day. Exactly at noon, the children fell to their knees, with chins turned upward, rain pouring onto their faces. They were obviously looking at and listening to something. Throughout the vision Mary prophesied things to come and instructions that must be followed. In the vision she identified herself as had been promised back on May 13th, saying, "I am the Lady of the Rosary," whom of course we know is Mary (most of the beads on a rosary are for the prayer Hail Mary).

Our focus here is on the prophecies that Mother

Mary delivered at Fatima and many other places and times throughout this century. To the Fatima children she confided the following:

The Prophecies of Fatima

1. Evil, sin and hell-like torment do indeed exist, despite the fashionable ideas to the contrary. Evildoers, sinners, abiders in hell and lost souls must soon begin to turn from their ways and catch hold of God's light and love, before it is too late. The children felt an ominous implication in all of this—something is going to happen, and it's going to happen soon. Everyone had better get his house in order and his heart right with God. Also, all seekers of God should pray for the conversion of evil and lost souls.

2. World War I will end within one year if you pray for peace and an end to war (spoken on 13 October 1917). WWI ended with the signing of an armistice on 11 November 1918.

3. The "war that was to end all wars" (WWI) would be followed by an even worse war. The evil of this war would be preceded by

a great light in the sky, which many in Europe saw. She also said the war would occur during the reign of a pope named "Pius XI" (specifically named by the Lady). At the time of this prophecy, the reigning Pope was Benedict XV. WWII began in 1936, during the reign of Pius XI.

4. In 1917 the Lady prophesied that a great battle for the heart of Russia would be waged. At this time in history, Russia was still a strong religious country, mostly Eastern Orthodox Catholic. The Lady said, "If Russia consecrates herself to the Immaculate Heart, then there will be peace. If not, then Russia will spread her errors throughout the world, bringing new wars and persecution. . . . Certain nations will be annihilated." All of us who have the benefit of hindsight know that Russia became the Soviet Union, gobbling up nations and peoples everywhere. Bolshevik-style Communism became the dark banner under which she traveled the world, creating her "Soviet Bloc." In 1917, Communism was simply a theory, not a threat, but the Bolshevik revolution was taking place in 1917. Little did the world know how powerful and menacing Bolshevik Communism

would become in future decades, right up until the fall of the Soviet Union in the 1980s. Since then religion is making a comeback in a broken and struggling Russia, and nations that had been gobbled up in the Union of Soviet Socialist Republic, are once again independent.

The Vatican has the entire prophecy but has refused to release it. Officials initially promised that they would release the complete prophecy in 1964, but did not, citing fears over the reaction to it. In 2001, Pope John Paul II released some of the Fatima prophecy. The portion he released dealt with assassination attempts against his own life, of which there have been two. He said that portions of the Fatima prophecy warned him of these and may have saved him from death. Now that some of the prophecy is being released, there is hope that, despite the terrible predictions that it may contain, the Vatican will let the people hear it for themselves and prepare as they see fit.

Garabandal, Spain, 1961

The entry for 18 June 1961 in thirteen-year-old Maria Concepcion Gonzalez's (nicknamed Conchita) diary reads as follows:

Suddenly there appeared to me a very beautiful figure that shone brilliantly but did not hurt my eyes at all. When the other three girls—Jacinta, Loli and Mari Cruz—saw me in this state of ecstasy, they thought that I was having a fit, because I kept saying, with my hands clasped: "Ay! Ay! Oh! Oh!" They were about to call my mother when they found themselves in the same state as I, and cried out together: "Ay! Oh! The angel!"

There was a short silence among the four of us. Then all of a sudden the angel disappeared and we returned to normal. Greatly frightened, we ran toward the church. As we passed the dance that was going on in the village, a girl named Pili Gonzalez said to us, "You look pale and scared!" We said together, "It is because we have seen an angel!" "Is it true?" she asked. We said together, "Yes, yes!"

Then we continued on in the direction of the church. When we arrived at the church, we went around back and cried. Some little girls playing there asked, "Why are you crying?" We said, "Because we saw an angel." They ran off to tell the schoolmistress.

When we stopped crying, we went into the church. The schoolmistress arrived in a very frightened state and asked us, "Is it true that you have seen an angel?" We simply replied, "Yes, yes." She then led us to a station [*this is the Stations of the Cross, a series of prayers before pictures of the various stages Jesus went through in his arrest, scourging, crucifixion, death and resurrection*], giving thanks to Jesus in the Blessed Sacrament.

When we finished the station, we all went home. My mother wanted me home before dark, but it was now nine o'clock and dark. She said, "Haven't I told you that you should get home while it is still daylight?"

I was very upset by these two things—having seen such a beautiful figure and having arrived home late. I don't dare go into the kitchen. I lean up against the doorpost and say, "I've seen an angel."

Mother says, "Coming home late, you come in here and tell me things like that!"

"But I did see an angel!"

We didn't say anything more about the matter that evening. The rest of the time was spent in the usual manner without talking about anything at all.

But the next day would prove to be a different situation. The word had spread all over town—

four hysterical girls had run to the church crying because they had seen something. Now the questioning and ridicule was to begin. Much of it occurred on the way to school by older children and adults. Once in school, however, their peers were very interested in all the details. School let out at one o'clock, and on their way home the town pastor caught up with them. He believed that they might have made a mistake in their assumption that it was an angel. Separating Conchita from the other children, he demanded that she be honest about this whole thing. But there was a nervousness about the priest that caused Conchita to recite every moment and detail of the event to him carefully. She noticed how attentively he listened. When she was done, he demanded that she ask the angellike being to identify himself—that is, if he came again.

The pastor questioned each of the other children separately, as he had Conchita. It was obvious to all that he was becoming more certain the children had seen something special. But he told everyone that he would wait to see if any more appearances occurred before he told the bishop.

The next days went by as most other days. Except for the visitors and the questions, life was normal—school, play and meals—until the girls desired to return to the spot. This caused their families to get upset. The overall feeling was to stay away from trouble, not to go looking for it. Conchita's mother started crying about "the mess." Life had been going just fine until this angel stuff. Conchita writes in her diary that she asked her mother to suppose it was true. "What then?" she asked. This reflection caused her mother to let her go.

Conchita called the spot "a corner of heaven" (*un trocito de cielo*). But on their way, the people made fun of the girls, asking "Why don't you go to the church to pray rather than that alley?" Some of the people actually tried to chase the children away, but they would not go. Then, as the children prayed, others began throwing stones at them. The children endured this, continuing to pray. After a long time, it became evident that the angel wasn't coming. As the children walked home, the schoolmistress met them and asked if they had been to the alley. When they explained that they had and that nothing had happened, she responded, as though it was common knowledge, that the angel hadn't come because it was very cloudy!

As the days passed without another appearance, more and more people began to think that it had all been the children's imagination—even the children themselves were beginning to wonder.

The original appearance had occurred at

about 8:30 P.M., but since it was summer, it was still light. On the evening of June 20th, the children happened to get together. So they decided to try again. In the alley they prayed their rosary and then, as they were leaving for their homes, a bright light began to shine. It was so bright that the children could no longer see each other. Unfortunately, they became frightened and began to scream. The brilliant light disappeared.

The next day, the children tried again. This time when the angel appeared, the children remained calm. They even asked him who he was and why he had come. He did not answer. The appearance was over shortly. But everyone watching the girls was now convinced that they were seeing something very special.

The evening of the 22nd, near the usual time, 8:30 P.M., the angel appeared again. The surrounding people only saw the children go into ecstasy. They saw no other phenomena. However, the expression on the children's faces caused an excitement to spread through the crowd, and the people began to shout, "*Era cierto!* (It's true!)"

As usual, the crowds attracted the police, and the police began to look for causes beyond the heavenly ones. Hypnosis was suspected and a charge was made against these girls and a man from the town who had been at the scene and who knew and practiced hypnosis. They wanted to put him in jail. But so many in the crowd were convinced that it was not hypnosis and testified that the man had nothing to do with the children before or during the appearance that the police took no action.

During the next appearance, which was a little earlier in the evening, many of the authorities were present. Their disbelief caused them to do many cruel things to these children. Conchita's own doctor lifted her up during the ecstasy (she was in a kneeling position) and dropped her from a height of three feet onto the stone street to see if she was faking it. There was a noise like cracking bones that caused many onlookers to cringe. Her legs remained bent in the kneeling position throughout the incident, and she landed on her knees. Obviously not aware of what had just happened to her, she remained in her ecstatic state. When she returned to normal consciousness, some concerned ladies began to examine and care for her knees.

Afterward the authorities took the children to the church, isolated them and began to interrogate them.

On the 26th and 27th, word had spread far and wide, and many people came to witness the angelic appearance. However, nothing happened. Disillusionment filled the crowd and the children. The believers were disappointed and the nonbelievers were filled with the pride of their certainty about things like this. Conchita remembers thinking, "If God wants it that way, that is the way it must be."

On the 28th, the angel appeared again, but this time at nine o'clock, and the ecstasy lasted until ten o'clock. The angel was very happy at the faith and persistence of the children and their supporters, but did not say this, or anything else. The children could simply sense his feelings. He appeared again and again over the next few days, until 1 July, when he finally spoke.

"Do you know why I have come?" the angel asked. "It is to announce to you that tomorrow, Sunday, the Virgin Mary will appear to you as Our Lady of Mount Carmel." The children replied, "We hope she comes soon!" The angel only smiled. Then the angel spoke with the children for two hours, which seemed like only a few minutes to the children.

Much of the conversation was friendly and casual, with the angel asking them if they remembered how concerned they had become when first they saw Conchita "have a fit" and were going to go get her mother? The children told the angel it was because she looked so strange. Then they all, including the angel, laughed. Finally, the angel said he would return tomorrow with the "Blessed Virgin."

Unlike the children's experiences at Fatima, the appearances of the angel at Garabandal caused the children great joy and uplifting. You'll recall the Fatima children, especially the youngest, felt great foreboding when in the presence of the angel. The Garabandal children only felt a great sadness after he had disappeared because they wished they could stay in his presence always.

During this appearance, the children noticed "a sign" that they had also seen in one of the previous appearances. Below the angel was a banner. On it were some words and below them were some Roman numerals:

It is necessary
that XVII—MCMLXI

In the previous appearance, the children simply did not want to take their eyes off the angel long enough to clearly see the banner. But in this appearance, they had plenty of time. They even asked the angel what it meant, to which he replied that the Virgin would tell them.

During this appearance the children also discerned more details of the angel's features and clothing. In her diary, Conchita describes him as follows:

The angel was dressed in a long, flowing blue garment without a belt. His wings were pale rose, long and very lovely. His little face was not long or round. His nose was very pretty. His eyes black and his skin dark. His hands were very delicate and his fingernails short. We did not see his feet.

On Sunday, 2 July 1961, the town was packed with people from all over. From the church, the girls and the crowd headed for the alley, but never made it. Along the way, around 6 P.M., the Blessed Virgin appeared with an angel on each side of her. One of them was the archangel Michael, whom the children knew. The other angel they did not recognize, but he was dressed exactly like Michael. The children thought they looked like twins. Next to the unknown angel was a large eye, which the children thought was the eye of God.

Conchita's dairy describes the Lady this way:

The Blessed Virgin appeared in a white dress, a blue mantle with a crown of small golden stars above her head. Her feet were not visible. Her hands were wide open. Her hair is long, dark brown and wavy, and parted in the middle. She has an oval-shaped face and her nose is long and delicate. Her mouth is very pretty with rather full lips. The color of her face is dark, but lighter than the angel's—it's different. Her voice is very lovely, a very unusual voice that I can't describe. There is no woman that resembles the Blessed Virgin in her voice, or anything else. In her arms she sometimes carries the baby Jesus. He is very tiny, like a newborn with a little face. His complexion is like that of the Blessed Virgin's.

From this apparition on, everyone close to the girls, including most of the townspeople and the pastor, believed and supported them. Their parents actually began to prepare and remind the children that the hour (6 P.M.) was approaching and they should get to the spot and begin praying. However, the children began to realize that in the past they were always "called" to come to the site. This was a surprise to everyone. The children explained that they "heard" an inner voice, but not with their ears, nor were their names actually called. In fact, there were three types of calling! One was a feeling of joy stirring within them. Another was stronger, with a noticeable sense of excitement rising within them. And the final and most powerful calling was a full, almost overwhelming feeling of excitement and happiness. The children said that they usually departed for the site on the second calling.

Not surprisingly, when the girls had finished describing the calls, they got a call! As is so common, the adult doubters still tried to test the girls.

They came up with a plan to separate the girls in different homes and then see if all four got the "calling" at the same time. A half hour after being separated, all four girls got the second calling at the same time and arrived at the new site of the apparitions at the same time. This really did amaze many of the doubters.

As soon as they arrived, the apparition appeared. It was 7 P.M. The Virgin Mary had the baby Jesus in her arms, but the angels were nowhere to be seen. Some of the people who had come with the children had given them objects for the Blessed Mother to kiss, and she kissed all of them. They asked to hold the baby Jesus, but both the baby and Mother only smiled at the request. She disappeared, saying, "Tomorrow you will see me again."

The kissed objects had the sweet scent of perfume about them. Everyone was excited. While the apparition was visible, the observers saw the girls playing with what appeared to be a baby, but they didn't actually see the baby.

It is interesting to note that the Garabandal girls never mentioned in their statements or journals any bright light or luminosity around the Blessed Mother. She appeared with clear form to her. However, the children do say that, though she kissed them good-bye, they never really felt physical contact against their heads, and when holding the baby they felt pressure but not physical contact. There was not a physical presence, or body, yet everything else seemed real.

On October 18th, we receive the first message from the Blessed Mother. Actually, the message was given to the children on July 4th, but they were to reveal it publicly after the apparition on October 18th.

She begins by asking them if they knew what the sign that the angel revealed to them meant. She told them it meant: "We must make many sacrifices, perform much penance and visit the Blessed Sacrament [*communion*] frequently. But first, we must lead good lives. If we do not, a chastisement will befall us. The cup is already filling up and if we do not change, a very great chastisement will come upon us."

After this apparition, the children wrote the message and signed it. All agreed that this was exactly what the Blessed Mother said. The children added, "The Blessed Virgin wants us to do these things, so that we may avoid God's punishment."

The Garabandal apparitions are many. They began in June 1961 and continued until November 1965. Throughout the recorded experiences and messages, there are prophecies. The first is about this "chastisement." The second is a "warning " (*el aviso*). And, the third is a "miracle"—Conchita was the only one to receive the miracle information and is to announce its coming eight days prior to the event.

The Miracle

By this time, many authorities were asking for a sign, a miracle. When the children asked the Blessed Mother to perform one for the doubters, she turned very grave and stopped smiling. Once, when a tape recorder had been brought to the scene, the children pleaded with her to speak onto the tape. Just as they were waiting for her to speak, the tape ran out; then an audible voice that everyone heard said, "I will not speak."

The miracle she prophesied is to occur in such a manner that the whole world will know it. Here is how Conchita describes it:

I am the only one to whom the Blessed Virgin spoke of the miracle. She forbade me to say what it will consist of. I can't announce the date either until eight days before it is due to occur. What I can reveal is that it will coincide with an event in the Church and with the feast of a saint, martyr of the Eucharist; that it will take place at eight-thirty on a Thursday evening; that it will be visible to all those who are in the village and surrounding mountains; that the sick who are present will be cured and the doubters will believe. It will be the greatest miracle that Jesus has performed for the world. There won't be the slightest doubt that it comes from God and that it is for the good of mankind. A sign of the miracle [*un señal del milagro*], which it will be possible to film or televise, will remain forever [*para siempre*] at the pines.

After reading Nostradamus's prophecy of Thursday becoming a Holy Day, Conchita's Thursday miracle is interesting. Could this miracle be the beginning of a new leader whose Holy Day will be recognized as Thursday because a great miracle occurred on that day at 8:30 P.M.? Certainly, if it is to be "the greatest miracle that Jesus has performed for the world," it's going to be a doozy, deserving of a special Holy Day. I thought raising Lazarus was a pretty good miracle. Of course, only a few dozen people saw that one.

When Conchita was asked to explain more about the sign that will remain at the Pines (an area in Garabandal where many apparitions took place), she said:

The sign that will remain forever at the pines is something that we will be able to photograph, televise and see, but not touch. It will be evident that it is not a thing of this world but from God.

As yet, Conchita has not gotten the message to alert us eight days before the miracle occurs.

The Chastisement

Conchita explains the chastisement this way:

The chastisement is conditional and depends on whether or not mankind heeds the messages of the Blessed Virgin and the miracle. If it should take place, I know what it will consist of because the Blessed Virgin told me about it, but I am not permitted to say what it is. Moreover, I have seen the chastisement. I can assure you that if it comes, it is worse than being enveloped in fire [*Van Allen Belts again?*], worse than having fire above and beneath you. I do not know how much time will elapse between the miracle and the chastisement.

If we do not change, the chastisement will be terrible in keeping with what we deserve. We saw it, but I cannot say what it consists of because I do not have permission from the Blessed Virgin to do so. I cannot say anything else about the chastisement. When I saw it, I felt a very great fear even though I was looking at the Blessed Virgin.

Interestingly, while the children were viewing the chastisement, many onlookers noticed how terrified they were, and began to pray. As soon as they did so, the children's cries and anguish subsided. But as soon as the onlookers stopped praying, the children immediately started crying and squirming as though suffering great discomfort.

The Warning

Conchita wrote that when the world sees the warning, the people will wish that they were dead rather than experience it. She goes on to say:

The Blessed Virgin told me on the first of January that a warning would be given before the miracle so that the world might amend itself. This warning, like the chastisement, is a very fearful thing for the good as well as for the wicked. It will draw the good closer to God and it will warn the wicked that the end of time is coming and that these are the last warnings. There is more to it than this, but it can't be said by letter. No one can stop it from happening. It is certain, although I know nothing concerning the day or the date.

Along with her statement, Conchita answered specific questions. Of the eighteen questions submitted to Conchita on 14 September 1965, four relate to the warning:

Q. Will the warning be a visible thing or an interior thing or both?

A. The warning is a thing that comes directly from God and will be visible throughout the entire world, in whatever place anyone might be.

Q. Will the warning reveal his personal sins to every person in the world and to persons of all faiths, including atheists?

A. Yes, the warning will be like a revelation of our sins, and it will be seen and experienced equally by believers and nonbelievers and people of any religion whatsoever.

Q. Is it true that the warning will cause many people to remember the dead?

A. The warning is like a purification for the miracle. And it is a sort of a catastrophe. It will make us think of the dead—that is, we would prefer to be dead than to experience the warning.

Q. Will the warning be recognized and accepted by the world as a direct sign from God?

A. Certainly, and for this reason I believe it is impossible that the world could be so hardened as not to change.

Finally Conchita says that the Blessed Mother told her that there would only be two more popes after Paul VI! Here are Conchita's own words on this:

> The Blessed Virgin said in 1962 that there will be only two more popes after Paul VI. But this does not mean that the world will come to an end.

Now we all know the papal prophecies of Malachy, the Monk of Padua, and Nostradamus's from previous chapters. This Garabandal prophecy does not seem to fit with these other prophecies of papal succession. The popes during the Garabandal apparitions were John XXIII (1958–1963) and then Paul VI (1963–1978). Using Conchita's statement, the current pope, John Paul II, would then be the last pope. Whereas Malachy, the Monk of Padua, and Nostradamus foresaw two more popes after the current one. We shall see.

ZEITOUN, EGYPT, 1968

The apparitions of the Virgin Mary over the Coptic Orthodox Christian Church in Zeitoun, an area in Cairo, Egypt, began in April 1968 and continued for the rest of that year. They are not formally recognized by the Roman Catholic

Church, but they have created a new spiritual
fervor among Coptic Christians.

Here is the official description by Father
Boutros Gayed, the rector of the church at the
time of the apparitions:

Zeitoun is a district within Cairo. Tumanbay
Street, where the Coptic Church is located, is a
main street in Zeitoun. Opposite the church
there used to be a big garage for the buses of
the Public Transport Authority. On 2 April
1968, an hour and a half after sunset, the me-
chanics and drivers of the garage were all
alarmed by some disturbance in the street. The
workmen ran to the street. They saw a young
lady dressed in white on the church dome. They
saw her walking on the dome. They thought
that she was about to throw herself down. So
they cried, "Be careful. Take care. You may fall
down. Wait." The dome is rounded and no
human being could walk on it. Then some of
the pedestrians who stood to watch the scene
cried, "Virgin Mary, Virgin Mary." The garage
workmen who were watching the apparition
were all Muslims. They looked on keenly and
they all became extremely astonished. The Blessed
Virgin, who appeared in a luminous body,
moved on the dome and bowed and knelt before the cross. The traffic in Tumanbay Street
was stopped and a big crowd of people stood

to watch the apparition of the Blessed Virgin. The workmen of the garage who were on duty at that particular time all gave reports that confirmed their witness, as they all gave the same particulars.

I have had the bliss of witnessing the Virgin's apparitions over the domes of the Church in Zeitoun. Rev. Father Costantin, the priest of the church, also saw the Blessed Virgin's apparition.

Sometimes only her head and shoulders appeared. At other times her full body appeared, moving between and on the domes. She bowed to the congregation and the crowds of people in front of the church. She blessed them. On certain nights she stood in the attitude of praying. She knelt in front of the church cross and the dome. Sometimes she was accompanied or preceded by celestial beings in the form of doves, luminous and bright. At other times she was seen with an olive branch in her hand.

The apparitions occurred throughout a whole year.

Other descriptions of these apparitions included the following:

The first appearance was in full luminous stature. She was wearing a long robe extending to below her feet. Sometimes she was surrounded by bright stars, and at other times she had a shawl about her head and her hands were extended forward.

The Virgin walked over the church, especially over the middle dome, and bowed in front of the cross that shone with a bright light.

She sometimes appeared with a babe in her arms. Other times she looked like a luminous shape over the eastern dome. Her features were clear.

The apparition of the Virgin was accompanied with, or preceded by, the appearance of white pigeons that used to circle the church. Sometimes a lightninglike light appeared. It shone for a while and then disappeared. Sometimes a luminous mist spread everywhere and gave off the strong, pleasant scent of incense, which pervaded the whole place. The apparitions lasted from a few minutes to as long as nine hours.

There was no audible message received by any onlookers, but all were moved by the spiritual apparition. Even Muslims who saw the apparitions chanted from the Koran: "Mary, God has chosen thee, and purified thee. He has chose thee above all women."

MEDJUGORJE, YUGOSLAVIA, 1981

These apparitions begin in a similar manner to those in Fatima and Garabandal. A seventeen-year-old girl sees a luminous silhouette suspended above the ground on a cloud and calls to her girlfriends, "Look, there's Our Lady, the Blessed Mother." Six children are involved in these apparitions, two boys and four girls. Most are sixteen and seventeen years old, but one is only ten. Most of the apparitions occur on or around a mountain, Mt. Podbrodo. As with other apparitions, the children see many wonders, encounter many stern and accusing adults and authorities, but endure to convince many of their sincerity. Onlookers also see miraculous phenomena, which help to support the belief that something special was happening.

Basically the luminous lady identifies herself as "The Mother of Peace," and explains:

I have come to tell the world that God is truth: He exists. True happiness and the fullness of life are in Him. I have come here as Queen of Peace to tell the world that peace is necessary for the salvation of the world. In God, one finds true joy from which true peace is derived.

At another time she says, "I have come because there are many believers here. I want to be with you to convert and reconcile everyone." She explains:

You know that I wish to guide you on the way of holiness, but I do not want to force you. I do not want you to be holy by force. I wish every one of you to help yourself and me by your little sacrifices so that I can guide you to be more holy, day by day. Therefore, dear children, I do not want to force you to live the messages; but rather, this long time I am with you shows that I love you immeasurably and that I wish every single one of you to be holy.

The Chastisement

The Queen of Peace gives the Medjugorje children ten "secrets." The children were told not to reveal the secrets until she gave them permission. It is known that some of the secrets deal with a chastisement that will come to the world. There is some uncertainty about whether this chastisement has already been averted or is yet to come. Apparently, the seventh secret prophesied a chastisement, but the eighth secret said that the chastisement had already been avoided because of world prayer. However, the ninth and tenth secrets each include chastisements. Now whether these are new chastisements or the same as those mentioned in the seventh secret is unclear to some writers. As I read the material, it appears they are new and different chastisements that are still to come. Perhaps one or both of them correspond with the chastisement the children saw at Garabandal.

Whatever the case, the Queen says that this chastisement can be mitigated "through prayer and fasting." She teaches that the world has lost its understanding of the value of prayer and fasting and that much can be changed by these practices. She explains:

> Pray with great meditation. Do not look at your watch all the time, but allow yourself to be led by the grace of God. Do not concern yourself too much with the things of this world, but entrust all that in prayer to Our Heavenly Father. . . . Avoid television . . . excessive sports, the unreasonable enjoyment of food and drink, alcohol, tobacco. . . . Definitely eliminate all anguish. Whoever abandons himself to God does not have room in his heart for anguish.

She encourages having "an encounter with God in prayer," a "meeting with God, the Creator." She says, "God gives Himself to you but He wants you to answer in your own freedom to His invitation."

The Sign

Another secret deals with a sign—a sign left by the Queen that the whole world will see. The children all claim to know when the sign or event is to occur. The sign is to appear on the apparitional hill. Its presence will be a call for mankind to return to God. "The Virgin said that there would be many more signs throughout the world before the great sign appears." But after the great sign appears, there will be no more time for "conversion." That is why the Virgin calls all to reconcile themselves with God now.

The Warning

Before the visible sign is given, there will come three warnings to the world in the form of singular events on earth "to allow people to return to God." Once the warnings begin, they will follow in short succession to one another. Enough time will pass between them to allow people to become sufficiently aware of each warning. During this period, many graces will pour out upon the people who seek attunement to God. This is reminiscent of many biblical prophecies:

Isa. 44:3 For I will pour water on the thirsty land, and streams on the dry ground; I will pour out my Spirit on your offspring, and my blessing on your descendants.

Ezek. 39:29   I will no longer hide my face from
them, for I will pour out my Spirit on the house
of Israel, declares the Sovereign LORD."

Joel 2:28   And afterward, I will pour out my
Spirit on all people. Your sons and daughters
will prophesy, your old men will dream
dreams, your young men will see visions.

Joel 2:29   Even on my servants, both men and
women, I will pour out my Spirit in those days.

Acts 2:17   In the last days, God says, I will
pour out my Spirit on all people. Your sons and
daughters will prophesy, your young men will
see visions, your old men will dream dreams.

Acts 2:18   Even on my servants, both men and
women, I will pour out my Spirit in those days,
and they will prophesy.

The Guidance

Throughout the Medjugorje apparitions, the
Queen gives much guidance as to what one
should be doing in these times. Here are two
examples:

Try to conquer some fault. If your fault is to
get angry at everything, try each day to get
angry less. . . . If you cannot stand those who

do not please you, try on a given day to speak
with them. If your fault is not to be able to
stand an arrogant person, you should try to approach that person. If you desire that person to
be humble, be humble yourselves. Show that
humility is worth more than pride.

You yourselves know what you have to do.
Make a decision for love. Love your neighbors.
Love those people from whom the evil is coming to you and so . . . you will be able to judge
the intentions of the heart. In the power of love
you can do even those things that seem impossible to you. . . . Hatred creates division and
does not see anybody or anything. Carry unity
and peace. Act with love in the place where you
live. Let love always be your only tool. With
love turn everything to good.

There is also a universality about the teachings from the Queen of Peace. As in this
teaching:

You must respect each man's beliefs. No one
should despise another for his convictions. God
is one and indivisible. It is not God but believers who have caused the dreadful divisions in
the world.

Mirjana, one of the six children, tells of being
taught by the Lady that devout Roman Catholics

go out of their way to avoid contact with Orthodox Catholics and Muslims; yet nobody who refused to take other believers seriously was
worthy of the name of Christian. The Lady sin-
gled out one of Mirjana's neighbors in Sarajevo,
a Muslim woman called Pasha. "She is a true
believer, a saintly woman. You should try to be
more like her."

As all of us now know, peace did not come
to Sarajevo. The dark influence prevailed and
the people chose "ethnic cleansing" rather than
cooperation, understanding and love.

RWANDA, AFRICA, 1981

Two rival tribes have been fighting in this little country since 1959, leading to all-out and
brutal civil war by 1990. A year before the apparitions began, pictures, statues and other icons
of the Virgin Mother were stolen, damaged or
destroyed in acts of iconoclasm that distressed
many of the faithful, who cried and prayed to
heaven for relief from this terror. It is thought
that this may have caused the apparitions to
begin in 1981.

Seven young people, from ages sixteen to
twenty-one, experienced visions of the Blessed
Mother separately, each seeing her personally,

never as a group. The visions lasted an hour or more, during which time the voice of the visionary was amplified somehow for the listening crowd to better hear—all in the native language of the Rwandans. Four of the young people were in a girls' boarding school. It was run by Rwandan Catholic nuns caring for children of any religion. In the following year (1982), the Blessed Mother appeared and spoke to five other girls from January to August. By December 1982 only a sixteen-year-old girl, Alphonsine, was still having visions. She continued to see the apparitions until January 1986! However, in 1989, on the anniversary of the first apparition, November 28th, Alphonsine saw the Blessed Mother one more time. The divine image told her that there would be no more appearances.

During these many apparitions, the image identified herself as "The Mother of the Word." This is a powerful title, referencing St. John's opening lines to his gospel:

John 1:1-5   In the beginning was the Word, and the Word was with God, and the Word was God. This One was with God in the beginning. Through this One all things were made; without this One nothing was made that has been made. In this One was life, and that life was the light of men. The light shines in the darkness, but the darkness has not understood it.

Normally, "this One" is translated "Him," but the original Greek is "this One." As we have discussed in the chapter of biblical prophecies, *Word* is the English translation for the Greek word *Logos. Logos* means much more than word. It is the essence of being, all consciousness. In Luke 21:33 Jesus uses *logos* once again when he says, "Heaven and earth will pass away, but My word will never pass away."

"The Mother of the Word" is calling us to attune ourselves to the Word, the Logos, and prepare for coming changes.

ASSIUT, EGYPT, 2000

The new millennium began with more apparitions in Egypt. The Virgin Mary began appearing above St. Mark's Coptic Christian Church in Assiut, Egypt, on 15 August 2000. Assiut is about halfway between Cairo and Luxor (about a five-hour drive from either city). People interpret these apparitions to be a response to a significant increase in tensions between Christians and Muslims in the region. The appearances have been going on for more than a year. People report seeing ghostlike doves and light flashes; then, after many hours, an apparition of a woman's form appears over the church. As with the appearances in Zeitoun, Egypt in 1968, no one reports hearing a message during the Assiut apparitions. However, Muslims and Christians alike join together at the site to view the apparitions. Perhaps this was the intended aim.

Hearing the Word of the Mother

In addition to the appearances of the Holy Mother, a more common phenomenon is that many people are claiming to be having "inner locutions," a term used to describe the hearing of a distinctive voice within ones consciousness—in these cases, it is the voice of the Virgin Mary. Others describe their Marian messages as coming by means of psychic channeling. Whatever the means, the messages received have a unifying theme, one was recently outlined in the popular book by Annie Kirkwood, *Mary's Message to the World*. In it, Mrs. Kirkwood says she "takes dictation from Mary," hearing her thoughts and then writing them on a computer word processor. Here is an example of one of Mrs. Kirkwood's inner messages from Mary:

Make sure you understand that this is not the end, but the beginning of a new era and a new world and a new understanding. The need to prepare is now, right before the birth of this new era.

All the apparitions of the Virgin Mary require some degree of faith on the part of those seeking to understand what it's all about and whether it really is Mary, the mother of Jesus. The parish priest at Lourdes, Father Dominique Peyramale, said, "For those who believe, no explanation is necessary. For those who do not believe, no explanation is possible." Maybe, but I'd like to attempt an explanation, or at least some elaboration.

THE DIVINE FEMININE

The most important element of this is a greater understanding of the entity involved. Who is this entity and what is her role in the big picture?

The Essenes were a monastic brotherhood of Jews living in Palestine from 2 B.C. to A.D. 2. It is wildely speculated that Jesus and his family were Essenes. The Essenes believed that God is both male and female in one, and that the Logos, the essence of being, is in this same image. Therefore, to them, there is a Divine Masculine and a Divine Feminine.

The Essenes believed that God meant what He

said when He turned to Eve as she and Adam were leaving the Garden and prophesied that out of her would come the Redeemer of the fall from grace. Therefore, the Essenes were preparing for the coming of the Messiah by looking for the "Eve" who would deliver Him. They knew that the Logos and the original Adam were male and female in one. It was only later that they were separated into Adam and Eve. Therefore, to the Essenes, the Messiah had to have a feminine component, and God had foreshadowed this in His prophecy.

There were several females in their Mt. Carmel temple that the Essenes thought might be chosen to fulfill Eve's destiny. One day a lady named Anne came to their temple. She told them that she was pregnant, but had not known any man. This was exactly what they had been looking for! In fact, some in the temple had actually considered Anne to be the female component of the coming of the Messiah. However, when she delivered a female child, some began to believe that even the feminine component had to be immaculately conceived since it was half of the Logos. Mary proved to be just that. While still very young and before she was married to Joseph, she conceived the Holy Child. Here is how Luke records their conversation:

Luke 1:26-41 In the sixth month, God sent the angel Gabriel to Nazareth, a town in Galilee, to

a virgin pledged to be married to a man named
Joseph, a descendant of David. The virgin's
name was Mary.

And coming in to her the angel said, "Hail,
O woman richly blessed! The Lord is with you."
Mary was greatly troubled at his words, and
kept pondering what manner of greeting this
might be.

But the angel said to her, "Do not be afraid,
Mary. You have found favor with God. Behold,
you will conceive in your womb and give birth
to a son, and you are to give Him the name
Jesus. He will be great and will be called the
Son of the Most High. The Lord God will give
Him the throne of His father, David, and He
will reign over the house of Jacob forever; His
kingdom will never end."

"How will this be," Mary asked the angel,
"since I am a virgin?"

The angel answered, "The Holy Spirit will
come upon you, and the power of the Most
High will overshadow you; for that reason the
holy one to be born will be called the Son of
God. Even Elizabeth, your relative, is going to
have a child in her old age, and she who was
said to be barren is in her sixth month. For
nothing is impossible with God."

"Behold, I am the servant of the Lord," Mary
answered. "May it be done to me as you have
said."

Then the angel left her.

At that time Mary got ready and hurried to

a town in the hill country of Judea, where she entered Zechariah's home and greeted Elizabeth. When Elizabeth heard Mary's greeting, the baby leaped in her womb, and Elizabeth was filled with the Holy Spirit. She cried out with a loud voice, "Blessed among women are you, and blessed is the fruit of your womb!"

What wonderful and powerful scenes. For the Essenes, the key insight comes in a verse that follows these. Elizabeth, filled with the Holy Spirit, speaks of the prophecy that the Essenes had held to so faithfully. She said:

Luke 1:45   Blessed is she who believed that there would be fulfillment of what had been spoken to her by the Lord.

"Fulfillment of what had been spoken to her by the Lord"—spoken when? To the Essenes, it was what was spoken to Adam and Eve by God as they were leaving the Garden. Out of Eve would come the Redeemer of this fall from grace. In Mary, the Holy Mother, this prophecy was fulfilled.

The Divine Feminine was prophesied to precede the coming of the Divine Masculine, and it did so. Perhaps the Virgin Mary's apparitions are in sync with a pattern. Perhaps this means that He will follow soon.

Notes

Chapter 1

1. See *A Commentary on the Revelation*, Edgar Cayce, published by A.R.E. Press.

2. See *After the End of Time: Revelation and the Growth of Consciousness*, Robin Robertson, Ph.D., Inner Vision Publishing.

3. See Matt. 4.

4. Heb. 2.

5. Matt. 22:21.

6. Matt. 17:26–27.

7. John 15:13.

8. See also Psalm 37:7.

9. 1 Kings 6:1.

10. 2 Kings 25:8.

11. Ezra 3.

12. 1 Cor. 15:52.

13. In Greek, it would be Christos or Christ. Messiah and Christos both mean "Anointed One."

Chapter 2

1. Their address and phone number are: A.R.E., P.O. Box 595, 67th St. and Atlantic Ave., Virginia Beach, VA 23451-0595, (757) 428-3588.

2. This is a clear reference to Jesus' comments in Matthew 24.

Chapter 3

1. See Cayce reading 281–33 for one example; there are many others.

2. The first number refers to the Century and the second to the quatrain.

3. Brennan, J. H., *Nostradamus: Visions and the Future*, 1992, Aquarian Press, London, p. 95.

4. *Ibid*, p. 100.

5. Matt. 24:12.

6. Roberts, Henry C., *The Complete Prophecies of Nostradamus*, 1947, Nostradamus Company, Oyster Bay, N.Y., p. 335.

7. Reading 294–151.

8. For more on this story read John Cornwell's *A Thief in the Night.*

9. See Rev. 20:7.

10. Reading 5748–6.

11. See Matt. 24:35.

12. More on this in Chapter 1.

13. See Matt. 24:19.